# The
# Flex-Continuity
# Basketball
# Offense

**Also by the author:**

*Basketball's Pro-Set Playbook: The Complete Offensive Arsenal*
*Complete Book of Zone Game Basketball*
*Coach's Guide to Basketball's 1-4 Offense*
*Pressure Game Basketball*
*Seven Championship-Tested Basketball Offenses*
*Tempo-Control Basketball*
*Successful Team Techniques in Basketball*

# The Flex-Continuity Basketball Offense

**HARRY L. "MIKE" HARKINS**

**Parker Publishing Company, Inc.**
**West Nyack, New York**

©1983, by

PARKER PUBLISHING COMPANY, INC.

West Nyack, N.Y.

Library of Congress Cataloging in Publication Data

Harkins, Harry L.
    The Flex-continuity basketball offense.

    Includes index.
    1. Basketball—Offense.   2. Basketball—Coaching.
I. Title.
GV889.H344   1983     796.32'32      82-22384
ISBN 0-13-322305-1

Printed in the United States of America

## Dedication

This book is dedicated to my wife, Grace, who, along with being the love of my life, has been a working partner in the books I have written. Without her meticulous efforts on the diagrams and hours spent typing, they might never have been completed.

# How This Book Will Help You

The Flex offense derives its name from the fact that it forces the defense to contract and then to expand. The first option makes the defense contract in order to cover a cutter inside the defense. The second option forces it to expand to cover an outside shot.

This pattern is an offspring of the three great continuity offenses. It features the expand and contract abilities of the Shuffle, the offside screen of the Reverse Action Pattern, and many of the rules of motion used in the Passing Game. The basic pattern is so simple that it is easily combined with other plays or offenses. It has more spontaneity than the Shuffle or the Reverse Action Pattern, and is more coachable than the Passing Game.

Another attribute of the Flex continuity is that it may be used successfully by a wide variety of personnel. The big team or big player can take advantage of the "post up" opportunities that are built into the pattern. Small teams or players can feature the continuous movement. The functional movement involved in the pattern neutralizes the pressure-help man-to-man defense and puts the defensive players at a rebounding disadvantage.

This is not an offense for helter-skelter, shot-forcing teams. It is designed for teams who seek a disciplined attack. This does not preclude running a fast break, but requires good shot selection, both on the break and when the team is running the pattern. It tests the defensive players physically and mentally. The basic plays provide continuous screens that test them physically. The discipline and shot selection force the defense to operate over an unusual period of time—and this tests its mental toughness.

The Flex is presented in the following manner:

## CHAPTER 1 — THE BASIC FLEX PATTERN

The book begins by explaining the basic movement. It describes the two basic plays around which the subsequent ideas are based. Also, in this chapter, coaching tips are given that help you in your job of teaching the offense.

## CHAPTER 2 — THE FLEX
## PLUS THE TRIANGLE OFFENSE

This chapter combines the Flex with the triangle offense. This gives a team the ability to either move the defense by way of the Flex or go inside with the triangle offense.

## CHAPTER 3 — THE FLEX PLUS THE DOUBLE STACK

This combination of plays allows you to test the defense with a myriad of play situations. In spite of the numerous options involved, this combination is easy to teach and the play keys are easy to read.

## CHAPTER 4 — THE FLEX PLUS SET PLAYS

This chapter features a well-integrated offense that contains the Flex and some often-used set plays. The team can run a quick-hitting set play or utilize the Flex movement.

## CHAPTER 5 — COMBINING THE
## FLEX AND PASSING GAME OFFENSE

Methods are provided that allow teams who want a lot of movement in their offense to use the Flex and passing game offenses in combination. Simple keys are used to facilitate the teaching of this plan. Coaching points are also provided that utilize the similarities in the offenses to help you present the ideas to your team.

## CHAPTER 6 — AUXILIARY PLAYS

Auxiliary plays are team techniques that may be added to take advantage of a particular situation. The objective may be to test an opponent's weakness or to take advantage of an apparent mismatch due to the ability of one of your players. They also may be added to give your offense more depth.

## CHAPTER 7 — PREPARING FOR ZONE DEFENSES WITH A FOUR-STEP PLAN

This chapter starts with the fundamentals of zone offense, suggests several simple zone plays, shows how the Flex can be adapted versus zones, and ends with a discussion of tempo-changing devices.

## CHAPTER 8 — THE DISCIPLINED FAST BREAK

Three fast-break patterns are presented that culminate in the Flex pattern. This is followed by an analysis of fast-break fundamentals.

## CHAPTER 9 — DEFEATING PRESSURE DEFENSES

Materials on both man-to-man and zone pressure offenses are included in this chapter. Some very current ideas are provided on playing against the run and jump defense, the man-to-man with a shortstop, and standard man-to-man and zone defenses.

## CHAPTER 10 — ANALYZING THE FLEX PATTERN

This chapter analyzes the Flex offense in regard to: how it allows for defensive balance, the high percentage shots provided, the rebounding plan, the amount of movement, the time factor, the individual initiative allowed, the play keys provided, its play components, how it adapts to zone defenses, how it meets pressure, and the way it encourages team effort.

This book provides a comprehensive look at the Flex offense. After detailing the basic pattern, it shows you:

- how to combine the pattern with other continuities.
- how to integrate set plays and the Flex pattern.
- auxiliary plays that may be added.
- methods of relieving defensive pressure.
- how to adapt the offense to zone defenses.
- methods of utilizing the fast break in conjunction with the pattern.
- drills that teach the offense.
- an analysis of the strengths and weaknesses of the offense.

The Flex is an easily learned combination of continuous basic plays. If used with discipline and patience, it will dissect the defense and will give your team the winning edge.

**Mike Harkins**

# ACKNOWLEDGMENTS

Grateful appreciation is expressed to the sources of my basketball knowledge, including:

Carroll Williams and Dick Edwards, the Flex pioneers.
Russ Estey and Mike Krino, my high school coaches.
Russ Beichly and Red Cochrane, my college coaches.
The players who have played on my teams.
And the publishers of *The Coaching Clinic, Scholastic Coach, Coach and Athlete,* and *Athletic Journal.*

A final note of thanks goes to my number one fans (and granddaughters) Shelle Ann and Jamee Cameron Harkins.

# CONTENTS

Step One: Stress the Fundamentals of Individual Zone Offense ... Step Two: Have an Uncomplicated Zone Offense ... Step Three: Adapt the Flex to Face Zone Defenses ... Flex Play #1 ... Double Stack (Three-Man Motion) ... Play #1: The Guard Through Three-Man Motion ... Guard Through Overshift ... Guard Through Overload ... Play #2: The Guard Choice Play ... Around the Double ... Around the Single ... Step Four: Sharpen Your Team's Tempo-Changing Techniques

Fast Break Pattern #1 ... The Middle Lane Option Pattern ... The Middle Open Option ... The Middle Jammed Option ... The Hookback Option ... The Long Pass Option ... Fast Break Pattern #2 ... The Runners' Lane Break ... Fast Break Pattern #3 ... The Forwards Run in Their Own Lanes ... Special Option ... Fast-Break Fundamentals ... The Outlet Pass ... Centering the Ball ... Organizing the Lanes ... The Control Area ... The Scoring Play ... Trailer Plays ... Center Trailer Lane ... Outside Lane Trailer Play ... Early Offense ... The Motivation Break

# 1. The Basic Flex Pattern

The "Flex" is a continuity offense that contains many of the properties of both the shuffle offense and the passing game offense. It provides functional movement that makes overplay difficult and virtually takes away the offside defensive help. The shot options offered by this pattern are from high percentage areas of the court.

## PERSONNEL ALIGNMENT

This continuity is run from a two guard, wide forward, single low-post set. Guards (1) and (2) line up at least two steps

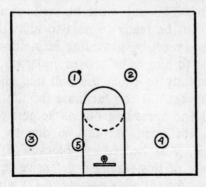

**DIAGRAM 1-1**

above the head of the key and as wide as the lane. Forwards (3) and (4) are told to play wide and not to crowd the post area. Post man (5) usually lines up on a plane as high as the forwards and, although it is not mandatory, on the ballside of the lane. See Diagram 1-1.

## THE BASIC MOVEMENT

The pattern of the Flex consists of two plays that may be run interchangeably. One is keyed by a guard-to-guard pass, and the other by a pass from guard to forward.

## PLAY #1
## GUARD TO GUARD KEY

This key may be read in two ways: (A) when the post is on the ballside and (B) when the post man is on the side opposite the ball.

### Ballside Post

When the post is on the ballside of the court and as a pass is made from guard (1) to guard (2) (Diagram 1-2), post man (5) steps out and screens for the ballside forward (3). Forward (3) then walks his defender into the screen, fakes high, and cuts low across the lane. This cut must be well-timed. If (3) goes too soon, (2) will not be ready to pass to him. If he cuts too late, the defense may react by providing help. Ideally, if (3) is open, (2) should pass to him as he arrives under the basket. This gives (3) the opportunity to catch the ball and shoot it while he is close to the basket. (3) can facilitate the timing of this pass by slowing down and spreading out as he gets to the basket.

If (3) is not open, it may be due to the fact that the defender on (5), (X5), hedged and blocked (3)'s cut. The offense takes advantage of this standard defensive technique by having (1) screen down for (5) after passing to (2), and (3)'s subsequent cut. Downscreener (1) must go right at (5)'s defender and make what passing game coaches call a "headhunter" screen. This is

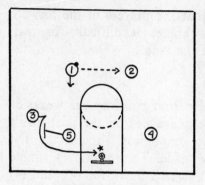

DIAGRAM 1-2

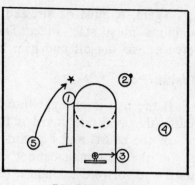

DIAGRAM 1-3

just another name for a definite solid, physical screen. This screen will often catch (X5) hedging or stepping out on (X3), and will provide (5) a clear cut to the free throw line for an unmolested jump shot. Player (5) must be careful not to move out high until (1) has set the screen. Otherwise, (X5) might be in motion and this would cause a "moving screen" foul to be called on (1). Note that when (3) did not receive a pass from (2), he cleared the lane to become the new man in the post on the opposite side. See Diagram 1-3.

When (5) receives the ball from (2) but is not open for a shot, the same motion is run, but on the opposite side of the court. (3) steps out to screen for (4) who cuts low to the basket. (2) downscreens for (3). See Diagrams 1-4 and 1-5.

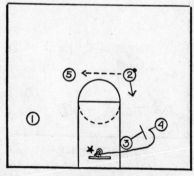

DIAGRAM 1-4

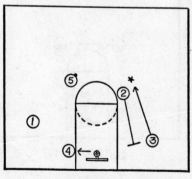

DIAGRAM 1-5

Again, it must be stressed that the players in the forward positions must stay wide. This makes it difficult for their defenders to sag off and help in the lane.

## Offside Post

If the ball is brought into the front court by the weakside guard (the weakside guard is the guard not on the post man's side of the court) and a guard to guard pass is made, the first cut off the post man cannot be made. The result is a simple guard and forward exchange. (2) screens down for (4), and (4) moves out front. See Diagram 1-6.

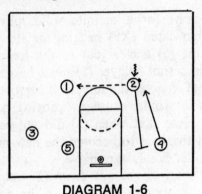

**DIAGRAM 1-6**

**DIAGRAM 1-7**

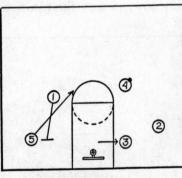

**DIAGRAM 1-8**

Then, if a pass were made from (1) to (4), it would be a strongside guard to weakside guard pass and would initiate the two basic cuts. See Diagrams 1-7 and 1-8.

A *special note* should be made now. Many coaches consider this Number 1 Play (guard to guard key) to be the Flex offense in its entirety. I feel that the addition of the following play makes the offense much harder to defense without making it difficult to teach.

## PLAY #2
## GUARD TO FORWARD KEY

The key for this play may also be read in two ways: (A) when the strongside guard passes to the strongside forward, and (B) when the weakside guard passes to the weakside forward.

### Strongside Key

In Diagram 1-9, guard (1) passes to forward (3). Both men in guard positions (1) and (2) screen away for the offside forward (4). Forward (4) moves to the ballside of the high post area looking for a pass from (3) and a possible jump shot.

This is also a good time for (3) to pass to (5) in the post because the offside defensive help is being kept very busy.

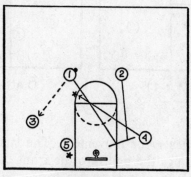

DIAGRAM 1-9

If (3) passes to (4) and a shot is not available, (1) loops around (2) and back out to the weakside guard area. Guard (2) then moves wide to the weakside forward position. See Diagram 1-10.

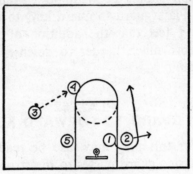

DIAGRAM 1-10

From there, (4) could initiate either a guard to guard play or another guard to forward play. See Diagram 1-11 and Diagram 1-12.

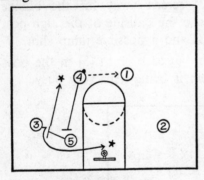

DIAGRAM 1-11

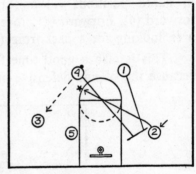

DIAGRAM 1-12

## Weakside Key

This option has *great* movement. The weakside guard (2) (Diagram 1-13) brings the ball into the front court and initiates the action by making a pass to his forward (4). Since it is a guard to forward pass, both guards will screen away. But before they do, the offside forward (3) cuts off post man (5) and to the ballside.

Guards (1) and (2) continue their screen away for (5), who cuts to the ballside high post area. See Diagram 1-14.

If (5) receives the ball and is not open, (2) loops around (1) and moves out front. From there a new option may be run. See Diagrams 1-15 and 1-16.

These two simple plays comprise the basic Flex offense. It is based on functional movement and composed of fundamental basketball maneuvers.

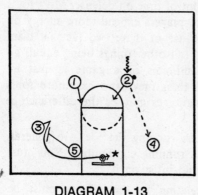

DIAGRAM 1-13

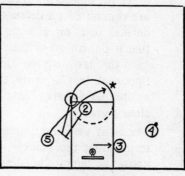

DIAGRAM 1-14

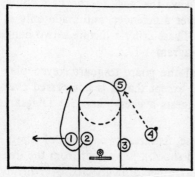

DIAGRAM 1-15

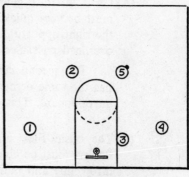

DIAGRAM 1-16

## COACHING TIPS FOR TEACHING THE FLEX

When introducing this offense, it will help if you use the following coaching tips:

- Discipline is a basic ingredient of a successful Flex offense. The players must be sold on the fact that most defenses are strong for three or four passes at the most. If the offense is wise in its shot selection and forces the defense to Flex, an obvious defensive lapse will occur.

- The players also should realize that it is smart basketball to make the opponents spend a lot of time on defense. Most fouls are committed on defense and players expend more energy on defense than on offense. Because of these two facts, a team that is patient on offense will (all other things being equal) go into the last two or three minutes of a game against an opponent that is more tired than they, and has more fouls against its players. These advantages may be the difference in close games.

- Tempo is very important when running the Flex. In general, teams move too quickly when running continuities. You must know the tempo you desire and insist on it.

- The correct fundamentals relating to the offense must be taught. Two examples would be:

  (A) On a guard-to-guard key, the pass to the first cutter must be very quick, over a defender, and made only at the right opportunity. These criteria dictate a two-hand overhead pass. See Diagram 1-17.

  The second cut of the guard-to-guard keyed play has the same demands except that it is not passed over an opponent. This suggests a chest pass. See Diagram 1-18.

  (B) The basic Flex offense features two types of shots. Players must be able to shoot a jump shot from the free throw line and make a rather difficult crossover layup from directly under the basket. Drills should be de-

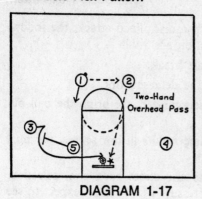

DIAGRAM 1-17

DIAGRAM 1-18

signed that offer these two shots and spot shooting should be part of each practice.

- Each player has strengths and weaknesses. One player may be instructed to score all his points off the pattern and another to seek one-on-one opportunities. The latter would be exemplified by a big man being told to "post up" after making the first cut on the guard-to-guard pass play.

- Many teams are running the passing game. It is an easy transition from the passing game to the Flex. You can point out that:

  A. Both offenses are continuities that require the man with the ball to pass in one direction and then screen away from the ball.

  B. The rule of not fighting pressure applies in both offenses. If you are overplayed and cannot receive a pass, don't stand still. Go through or go back and screen for a teammate.

  C. The passing game rule of not taking any shot but a layup until five passes are made is also appropriate for the Flex offense.

- Since the Flex offense is such a disciplined attack, the following team principles of operation are vital:
  - We do not force the fast break.
  - We believe in making the defense work.
  - When our offense is disorganized, we bring the ball out front and start over.
  - Because our type of game results in low scores, we must play strong defense.
  - Since we take our time and stress good shot selection, teams will attempt to pressure us. We must expect to see a lot of pressure defenses.
- The final selling point for the Flex offense is that the above ideas represent the way most teams play in the latter part of very close games. You should point out that if your team uses these principles at all times, it will have the advantage in close games.

# 2. The Flex Plus the Triangle Plan

The Flex plus the triangle plan is another example of an offense that thoroughly tests the defensive perimeter (by way of the Flex) and also provides inside pressure on the defense (by way of the triangle). Together they present the defense with a myriad of problems.

## PERSONNEL ALIGNMENT

The initial personnel alignment consists of guards (1) and (2). Guard (1) is a dribbling, quarterback-type and (2) is a tall, all-around player, who can help bring the ball up court and then play well inside.

Forward (3) is stacked inside post man (5). He can be smaller than an average forward, but he should be a good shooter and passer.

Forward (4) should be the bigger of the forwards and at least an average shooter. It also helps if he has some ability in the pivot.

Post man (5) should be big, strong, and an average shooter or better. See Diagram 2-1.

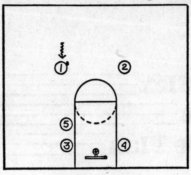

DIAGRAM 2-1

## THE TWO PLAY KEYS

As (1) dribbles up court and the guards reach the area just above the head of the key, (3) pops out as (5) screens down. At the same time, (2) screens down for (4). (1)'s pass will key either the Flex or the triangle movement. If (1) passes to (4), it keys the Flex. See Diagram 2-2.

If (1) passes to (3), it keys the triangle movement. See Diagram 2-3.

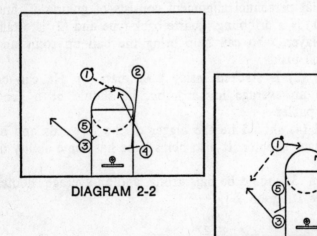

DIAGRAM 2-2

DIAGRAM 2-3

## THE FLEX

As soon as (1) passes to (4), (3) cuts off (5), who has stepped out to screen for him. (1) then screens down for (5) and the basic Flex play #1 is in operation. See Diagrams 2-4 and 2-5.

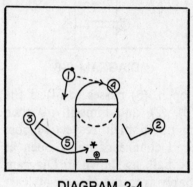

DIAGRAM 2-4

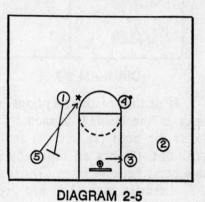

DIAGRAM 2-5

## THE TRIANGLE PLAY

When (1) passes to (3), he clears to the offside wing position, and (4) makes his cut to the top of the key. Player (5) posts up, and (3) may shoot or pass to (5). See Diagram 2-6.

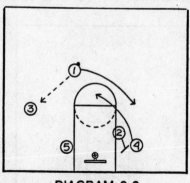

DIAGRAM 2-6

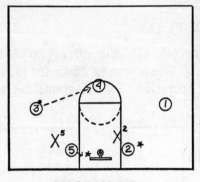

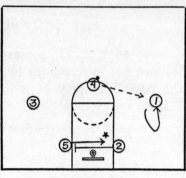

**DIAGRAM 2-7**                    **DIAGRAM 2-8**

If neither of these options is open, (3) passes to (4) at the apex of the triangle formed by (5), (2), and himself. (4) then looks for both (5) and (2) setting up in their respective post positions. (5) has an especially good chance of being open at this point because when (3) had the ball, as shown in Diagram 2-7, defensive man (X5) was probably fronting (5), or at least was in a strong overplay position. This might permit (4) to lob to (5) for an easy layup.

If (5) or (2) is not open, (4) passes to (1) or back to (3). This tells the ballside post man (2) in Diagram 2-8 to screen away for the offside post man (5), who moves to the ball.

In Diagram 2-9, (5) is not open so (4) screens down for (2), who had just screened for (5). (2) cuts to the high-post area

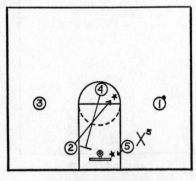

**DIAGRAM 2-9**

previously occupied by (4). This offside action takes away the defensive help and may allow (1) to lob to (5).

At times, (5) will be fronted and if (1) passes to (2), (2) may be able to get the ball to (5) inside the defender (X5). See Diagram 2-10.

In most cases, though, when (2) receives the ball from (1), (4) and (5) post up and (2) attempts to get the ball to either of them. See Diagram 2-11.

(4) and (5) can facilitate this pass by extending the elbow nearest their defensive man and giving (2) a target with their other hand.

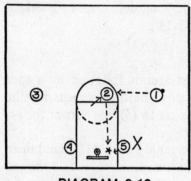

DIAGRAM 2-10

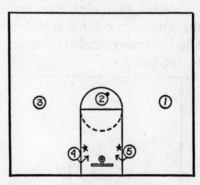

DIAGRAM 2-11

If this pass cannot be made, (2) passes to either (3) or (1) and the same triangle rotation is repeated. Note that (1) and (3) faked to the baseline and then cut toward the ball. This move

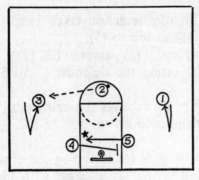

**DIAGRAM 2-12**

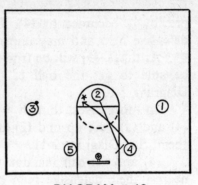

**DIAGRAM 2-13**

makes it much more difficult for the wing defenders to intercept this pass. See Diagrams 2-12 and 2-13.

### Split Option

Any pass to a man in the post area is followed by a split play. If a wing man passes to the post, he then screens for the man in the point position. See (3) pass to (5) and screen for (4) in Diagram 2-14.

Note that (3) rolled after screening and (1) maintained defensive balance by moving to the point.

When the point man passes to a post man, he screens for the wing man on that side. Note in Diagram 2-15 that (4) rolled after screening, and (1) maintained defensive balance by moving to the point.

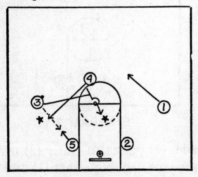

**DIAGRAM 2-14**

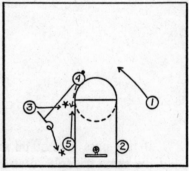

**DIAGRAM 2-15**

When playing against extreme overplay defenses, a backdoor option may be added. In Diagram 2-16, when (4) passes to (5), wing man (3) backdoors his defender and cuts to the ballside layup area.

If (3) is not open, he stops and waits for (4) to come down and screen for him. (4) screens and rolls and (3) cuts to the ball. See Diagram 2-17.

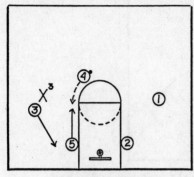

**DIAGRAM 2-16**

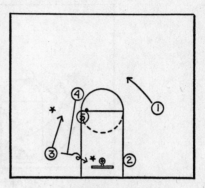

**DIAGRAM 2-17**

After rolling, (4) clears the layup area and moves across the lane and around (2). This affords (5) the room to make a one-on-one play. See Diagram 2-18.

This splitting movement, along with providing scoring options, keeps the defense busy and gives the post man room to work.

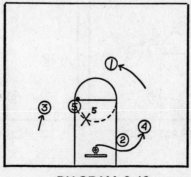

**DIAGRAM 2-18**

## DRIBBLE CHASE (Point to Wing)

At times, the defense will deny the point to wing pass. As shown in Diagram 2-19, point man (2) cannot pass to either wing, so he dribbles at wing man (3) and clears him down and around the two post men to the offside wing area. Offside wing man (1) then takes the point.

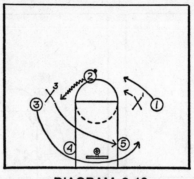

DIAGRAM 2-19

(2) can now pass to (4) in the low-post area or to (1) in the high-post area. If the pass is to (1), he looks inside and then passes to either wing man. (1) passes to (3) and the triangle rotation again takes place. (See Diagrams 2-20 and 2-21).

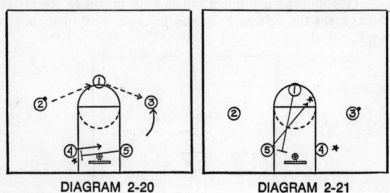

DIAGRAM 2-20                    DIAGRAM 2-21

## DRIBBLE CHASE (Wing to Point)

When a wing man cannot pass inside and the point man is being overplayed, the wing to point dribble chase may be used. In Diagram 2-22, wing man (3) dribbles at point man (1), who clears down and around the ballside post man (4) to replace (3) at the wing position.

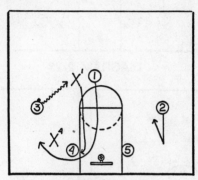

**DIAGRAM 2-22**

Note that as this dribble chase is run, the offside wing man makes a move to get open. (3) may then pass to either wing and another triangle rotation would be run.

## PATTERN SET

If further offense is desired, plays may be added that lead into the formations of the Flex and triangle plays. These are called *pattern set plays.* An example run from a 1-2-2 triangle set would be:

### Keying the Flex with a Screen and Roll

This play begins as point man (1) dribbles off post man (4). This tells (4) to roll to the basket and the offside post man (5) to screen away for (3), who comes out front. See Diagram 2-23.

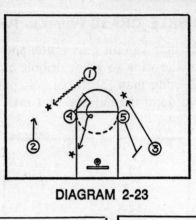

DIAGRAM 2-23

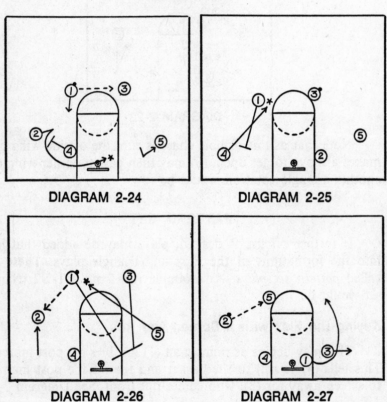

DIAGRAM 2-24                    DIAGRAM 2-25

DIAGRAM 2-26                    DIAGRAM 2-27

(1) can shoot, look for (4) rolling to the basket, or start the Flex play #1 by passing to (3). See Diagrams 2-24 and 2-25.

(1) could have keyed Flex play #2 by passing to (2). See Diagrams 2-26 and 2-27.

## Keying the Triangle with a Backdoor Play

This play begins in the same manner as the key to the Flex, but player (5) keys the triangle sequence by breaking to the high-post area once the screen and roll has been made. See Diagram 2-28.

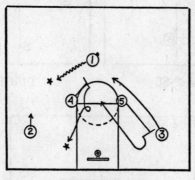

DIAGRAM 2-28

(1) then passes to (5), (3) backdoors his defender and goes to the low-post area, and (1) follows his pass and goes to the offside wing area. See Diagram 2-29.

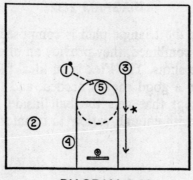

DIAGRAM 2-29

The team is now in position to run the triangle sequence shown in Diagrams 2-30 through 2-32.

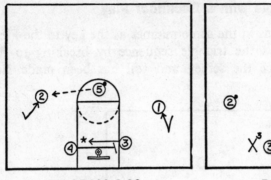

DIAGRAM 2-30

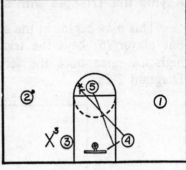

DIAGRAM 2-31

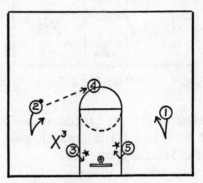

DIAGRAM 2-32

The Flex plus the triangle plan is composed of very simple maneuvers. When combined, they provide an offense that results in high percentage shots. The Flex is an ideal play to take time off the clock when a good shot is needed, and the triangle is a quick-hitting concept that gets the ball inside. Together, they offer a team plan with enough variety to counter most defensive situations.

# 3. The Flex Plus the Double Stack

The Flex plus the double stack offense provides a series of play situations that present the defense with a wide range of problems. The Flex can be featured when movement is desired and the double stack is a method of stressing the inside game.

## PERSONNEL ALIGNMENT

This offense starts from a double stack alignment. As shown in Diagram 3-1, (1) is the point man and wing men (2) and (3) are stacked inside the two biggest players, (4) and (5).

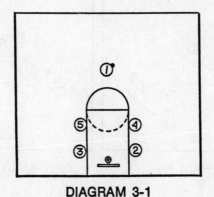

DIAGRAM 3-1

## PLAY KEYS

From this starting set, either the Flex or the stack may be keyed. The double stack is keyed when (5) and (4) screen down for (3) and (2) and then roll inside to the post area. See Diagrams 3-2 and 3-3.

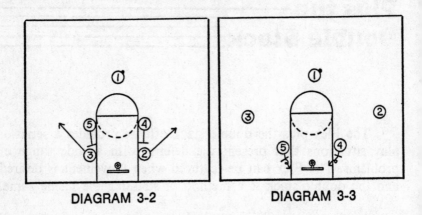

DIAGRAM 3-2                          DIAGRAM 3-3

The Flex is also keyed after (4) and (5) screen down for (2) and (3). This time, however, the ballside post man (5) clears to the ballside corner. See Diagrams 3-4 and 3-5.

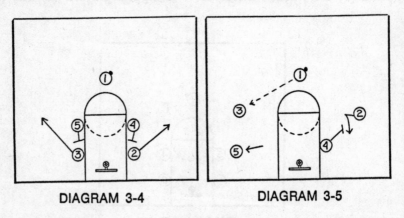

DIAGRAM 3-4                          DIAGRAM 3-5

## THE FLEX

Once (5) has cleared to the corner, the offside wing man (2) cuts off the offside post man (4) and to the ballside low-post area. See Diagram 3-6.

(1) then screens down for (4) and the Flex pattern is in operation. See Diagram 3-7.

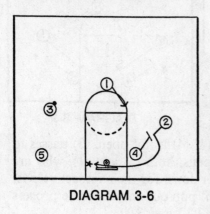

DIAGRAM 3-6

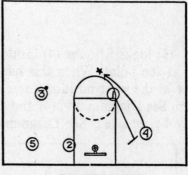

DIAGRAM 3-7

## THE DOUBLE STACK

The double stack play may be run in three ways. These include a five-man motion, a four-man motion, and a three-man motion.

### The Five-Man Motion

(2) and (3) pop out from the downscreens of (4) and (5). In Diagram 3-8, (1) passes to (3). This tells (5) to screen away for (4) and (1) to screen away for (2). (4) comes to the ballside low-post area, and (2) comes to the point.

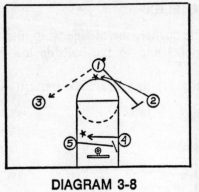

DIAGRAM 3-8

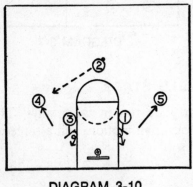

DIAGRAM 3-9

(3) looks first for (4) inside. If (4) is not open, (3) passes to (2) at the point. When this happens, both (3) and (1), who are now at the wing positions, screen down for their respective post men. See Diagram 3-9. (4) and (5) pop out and the same process may be repeated. See Diagrams 3-10 and 3-11.

DIAGRAM 3-10

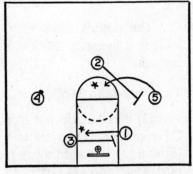

DIAGRAM 3-11

## Four-Man Motion (Double Stack)

If a team has a very strong rebounder, they may choose to combine the Flex with the four-man double stack motion. The strong rebounder plays in the (4) position. In Diagram 3-12, (2) and (3) pop out from the downscreens of (4) and (5). (3) receives the pass from (1). When running the four-man motion, the onside post man (5) does not screen away. He sets up in the low-post area and (3) attempts to get him the ball. The offside post man (4) then cuts to the ballside high-post area. See Diagram 3-13.

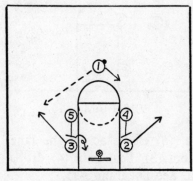

DIAGRAM 3-12

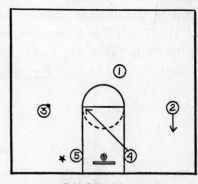

DIAGRAM 3-13

Player (3) may now pass inside to (5). He may also pass to (4), who looks for the shot. If (5) is being fronted, (3) passes to him inside his defender, (X5). See Diagram 3-14.

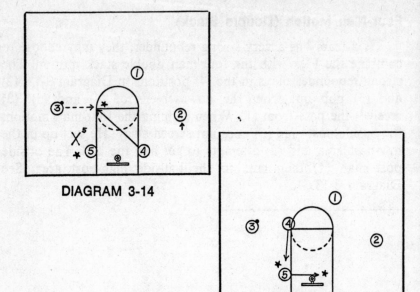

DIAGRAM 3-14

DIAGRAM 3-15

If neither (4) nor (5) is open, (5) clears across the lane looking for a possible lob pass from (3). Post man (4) drops down to the ballside low-post area. See Diagram 3-15.

If (4) or (5) is still not open, (1) screens away for (2), and (3) passes to (2) at the point. See Diagram 3-16.

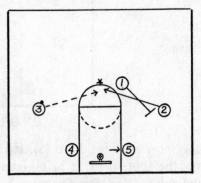

DIAGRAM 3-16

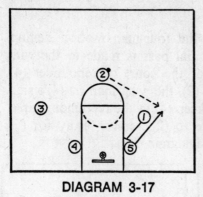

DIAGRAM 3-17

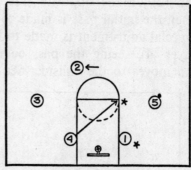

DIAGRAM 3-18

Point man (1) then downscreens for (5), who has cleared the lane. Post (5) pops out of (1)'s downscreen and (2) gets the ball to him. See Diagram 3-17. From there, the same process is repeated. See Diagrams 3-18 through 3-20.

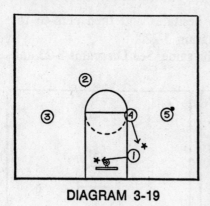

DIAGRAM 3-19

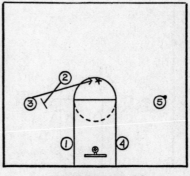

DIAGRAM 3-20

## Special Note

The following example of the four-man motion demonstrates what occurs when the initial pass is made to the wing man (2) on the opposite side of the court of rebounder (4). When the initial pass is made to (2), the wing man on (4)'s side, a special adjustment is made to keep (4) in the rebounding area. Player (4), seeing the pass come to (2), screens away for (5), who moves to the ballside. See Diagram 3-21.

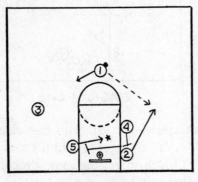

DIAGRAM 3-21

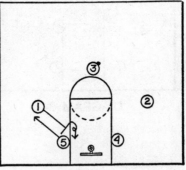

DIAGRAM 3-22

After screening for (5), (4) hesitates and then cuts to the ballside high-post area. See Diagram 3-22.

From there, the pattern is the same. See Diagrams 3-23 and 3-24.

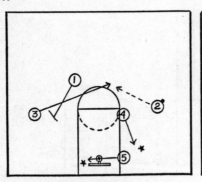

DIAGRAM 3-23

DIAGRAM 3-24

The four-man motion permits the strong rebounder, (4), to stay close to the basket, and the other four men to interchange positions.

## Three-Man Motion (Double Stack)

The three-man motion works well for the team that has a very small man, (1), whom they wish to keep back on defense and a strong rebounder, (4). It is also an excellent zone motion.

Point man (1) passes to either (2) or (3) as they come out of the downscreens of (5) and (4). In Diagram 3-25, (1) passes to (3), (5) posts up, and the offside post man, (4), breaks to the ballside post area. Player (3) may pass to (5) low, to (4) breaking high, or reverse the ball by way of the point man, (1). In the three-man motion, (1) does not screen for the offside wing man. He stays at the point.

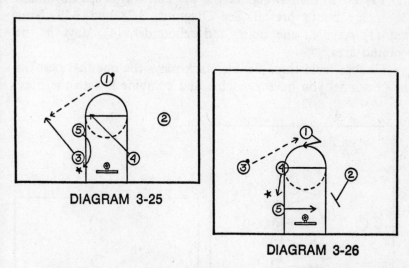

DIAGRAM 3-25

DIAGRAM 3-26

Player (5) then moves across the lane looking for the lob pass, and (4) drops down to the ballside low post. In order to get open for (3)'s pass, (1) fakes away and comes back to the ball. As (1) receives the ball out front, (2) screens down for (5). See Diagram 3-26.

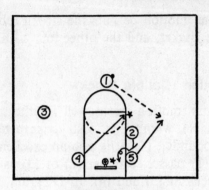

**DIAGRAM 3-27**

In Diagram 3-27, (5) uses (2)'s downscreen to get open. He receives the ball from (1), looks first for (2) in the post, and then for (4) breaking to the ballside high-post area.

Player (2) then swings across the lane, (4) drops down and the same options prevail. See Diagrams 3-28 and 3-29. Note that (1) stays at the point and rebounder, (4), stays in the rebound area.

Choose from these double stack plays the one that best fits the personnel you have available and combine it with the Flex.

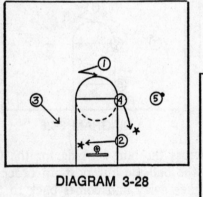

**DIAGRAM 3-28**

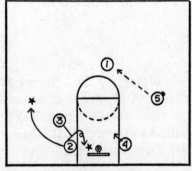

**DIAGRAM 3-29**

## Initiating the Five-Man Double Stack Motion from the Flex Pattern

It is possible to be running Play #1 of the basic Flex offense and quickly switch to the double stack five-man motion. This is done when the offside forward (4) (Diagram 3-30) pinches in and allows (3) to loop around him.

Now the point man is (2), as (1) screens down for (5), as per the Flex. The result is a double stack formation from which any of the three double stack motions may be run. See Diagram 3-31.

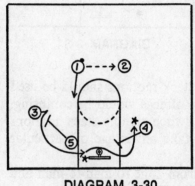 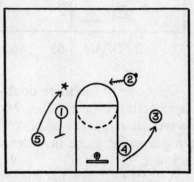

DIAGRAM 3-30          DIAGRAM 3-31

Point man (2) can now pass to either wing (5) or (3) and start the double stack motion. Diagram 3-32 shows the start of the five-man motion.

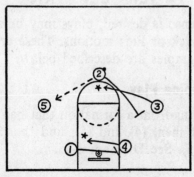

DIAGRAM 3-32

Diagram 3-33 shows the start of the four-man motion. Diagram 3-34 shows the start of the three-man motion.

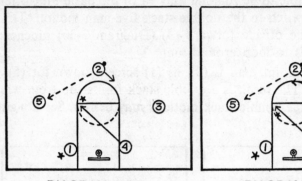

DIAGRAM 3-33              DIAGRAM 3-34

Only one of the three double stack motions should be used in conjunction with the Flex. More offense would be confusing. However, it might be possible to switch double stack motions for a particular game in order to take advantage of particular match-ups.

Against defenses that change from zone to man-to-man and back, it might be wise to use the Flex plus the three-man motion. The three-man motion is an excellent zone offense. This same plan is also effective against combination defenses.

## PATTERN SET PLAYS

If further offense is desired, plays may be added that lead into the double stack or Flex motions. These are called *pattern set plays.* Two examples are described below.

### I. The Guard Choice Play

This play begins from a formation that has two guards, (1) and (2); two post men, (4) and (5); and the (3) man stacked under post man (5). See Diagram 3-35.

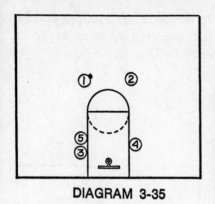

DIAGRAM 3-35

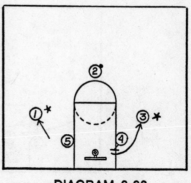

DIAGRAM 3-36

The play begins as guard (1) passes to guard (2) and cuts down the lane. See Diagram 3-36.

Player (1) may now make either of two cuts:

A. He may cut around the wall formed by players (5) and (3). When this happens, (3) cuts opposite (1) and loops around (4), who screens down. See Diagrams 3-37 and 3-38.

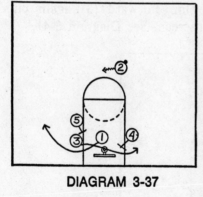

DIAGRAM 3-37

DIAGRAM 3-38

From there, either the Flex or double stack motions can be keyed by a pass to either wing man. See the Flex being keyed in Diagram 3-39, and the double stack in Diagram 3-40.

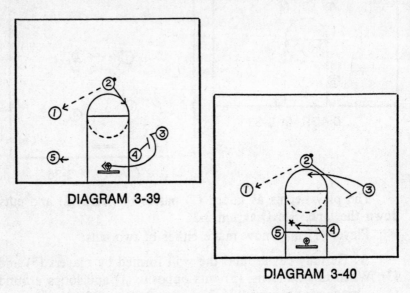

DIAGRAM 3-39

DIAGRAM 3-40

B. Player (1) may choose to cut around the single man (4), who would screen down for him. Forward (3) again cuts opposite (1) by using (5)'s downscreen. See Diagram 3-41.

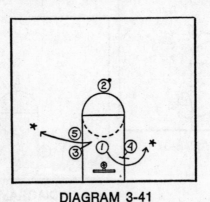

DIAGRAM 3-41

Again either the Flex or double stack motions may be keyed after a pass to either wing man. See the Flex being keyed in Diagram 3-42, and the double stack being keyed in Diagram 3-43.

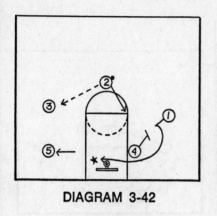

**DIAGRAM 3-42**

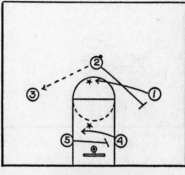

**DIAGRAM 3-43**

## II. The Basic Outside Cut Lob Play

This play begins when guard (1) passes to forward (3) and makes an outside cut. This tells the offside forward (4) to come across the lane. See Diagram 3-44.

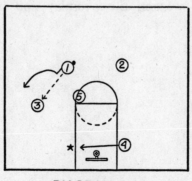

**DIAGRAM 3-44**

Forward (3) returns the ball to (1) and cuts over post man (5) for a possible lob pass. See Diagram 3-45.

If (3) is not open, (1) dribbles off (5), who rolls to the basket and screens for (4). At the same time (2) screens down for (3). See Diagram 3-46.

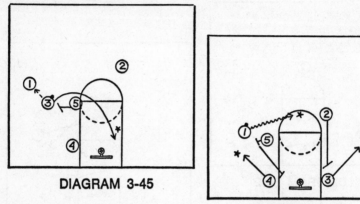

DIAGRAM 3-45

DIAGRAM 3-46

Player (3) may shoot or pass to (4) or (3), and start either the Flex or the double stack.

With the advent of the pressure and help man-to-man defense, motion became the key word on offense. Using the Flex in combination with the double stack provides the movement necessary to weaken the overplay and immobilize the defensive help.

# 4. Combining the Flex with Set Plays

This adaptation of the Flex pattern allows a team to run the pattern, but still take advantage of a strong post man.

## PERSONNEL ALIGNMENT

This variation of the Flex has an unorthodox alignment. The two guards (1) and (2) are wide enough that their end of the free throw line is between them and the basket. The lead guard is (2). The ballside forward (4) is as high as the free throw line extended. The post man is low on (4)'s side. The offside forward cuts to the high-post area in the middle of the free throw line. See Diagram 4-1.

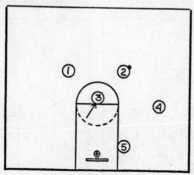

DIAGRAM 4-1

55

## PLAY #1
## OUTSIDE CUT

When (2) passes to (4), he makes an outside cut to the ballside corner. At the same time, the offside guard (1) cuts toward the ball and then to the basket utilizing (3) for a blind screen. Player (4) looks to (1) for a possible lob pass. See Diagram 4-2.

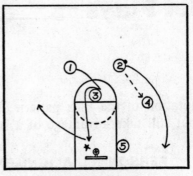

DIAGRAM 4-2

If (1) is not open, he flares to the offside wing area. From there, (4) can key the following options.

### Split Option

Player (4) passes to post man (5) and splits the post with either (2) in the corner or (3) in the high post.

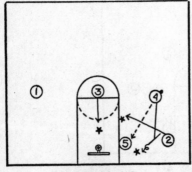

DIAGRAM 4-3

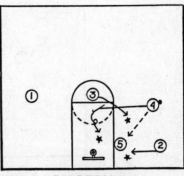

DIAGRAM 4-4

In Diagram 4-3, (4) splits with (2) and (3) backdoors.

In Diagram 4-4, (4) splits with (3) and this tells (2) to backdoor.

Another option that arises is when (4) attempts to pass to (5) and he is fronted. There is no defensive help on a lob pass and (5) has an unmolested power-up shot. See Diagram 4-5.

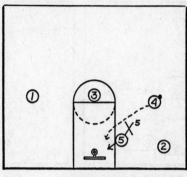

DIAGRAM 4-5

## Corner Option

Player (4) may pass to (2) in the corner and key the corner option. When this happens, (4) cuts between (5) and (2), (5) steps out and he and (2) work a screen and roll play. See Diagrams 4-6 and 4-7.

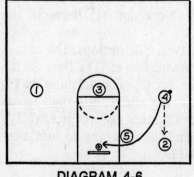

DIAGRAM 4-6

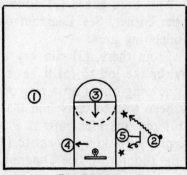

DIAGRAM 4-7

## The Flex Option

Player (4) may decide not to run one of the set plays and key the Flex. He does this by passing to (3) in the high-post area. When this happens, (5) steps out to screen for (2), who cuts to the basket. See Diagram 4-8.

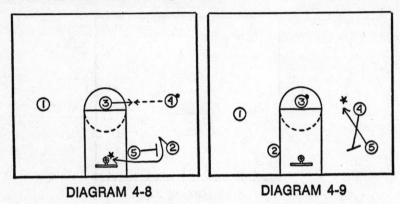

DIAGRAM 4-8                         DIAGRAM 4-9

If (2) was not open, (4) would screen down for (5) and the guard to guard phase of the Flex pattern would be run. See Diagram 4-9. From there, the pattern would continue.

## PLAY #2
## DRIBBLE ENTRY

This time guard (2) dribbles at forward (4) and clears him to the corner. See Diagram 4-10. Note that (1) flares to the offside wing area.

From there, (2) can key the two split options, the corner play, or the lob to (5) if he is fronted. Player (1)'s flare to the offside wing opens up a new option for (3). The defender on (3) has been told to deny him the ball. He also knows that a pass to (3) keys the Flex pattern. Player (2) takes advantage of (X3)'s overplay by faking a pass to (3) and then lobbing to him after he backdoors (3). See Diagram 4-11.

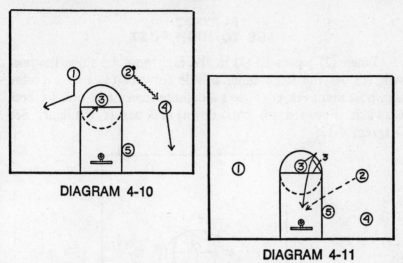

DIAGRAM 4-10

DIAGRAM 4-11

If (3) is not open, (2) does not make the pass. Player (1) replaces (3) in the high post and (3) flares to the offside wing. See Diagram 4-12.

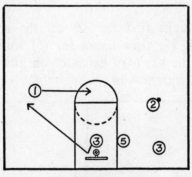

DIAGRAM 4-12

From there, all the options may be run. A pass to (1) would key the Flex. A pass to (3) in the corner would key the corner screen and roll. A pass to (5) would lead to a split play. The ball could be lobbed to (5).

## PLAY #3
## PASS TO HIGH POST

When (2) passes to (3) in the high post, he splits the post
with (1). At the same time, offside forward (4) cuts over the
high post man. Player (5) sets a definite screen and tries to force
a switch. Forward (4) cuts down and across the lane. See
Diagram 4-13.

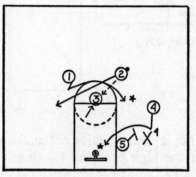

**DIAGRAM 4-13**

Player (3) looks first for (2) off the split, then for (4)
coming over (5). He then looks for (5) rolling inside. If (5)
forced a switch, he has (4)'s defender on him and it may be a
mismatch. See Diagram 4-14.

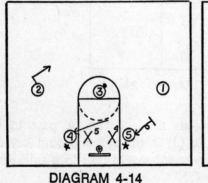 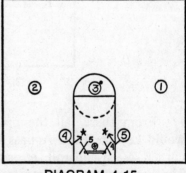

**DIAGRAM 4-14**          **DIAGRAM 4-15**

Player (3) holds the ball above his head and both (5) and (4) post up. See Diagram 4-15.

## PLAY #4
## PASS TO LOW POST

When (2) chooses to bounce pass to (5) in the low post, he then cuts away and over (3) for a possible return pass. Guard (1) uses (2)'s cut to come to the ball and the onside forward (4) backdoors his man. See Diagram 4-16.

Player (5) hits the open man or makes a one-on-one play.

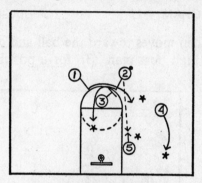

DIAGRAM 4-16

## CHANGING SIDES

This lopsided formation is usually run on the same side, but occasionally it is desirable to change sides. This is usually done in one of the following two ways.

### A. Pass to the Weakside Guard

When the lead guard (2) passes to (1), it keys a change of side. Guard (1) dribbles to the wing area on his side. The former strongside forward (4) cuts off the post man (5), and may be open under the basket. See Diagram 4-17.

If (4) is not open, he continues to the ballside corner, and (5) swings to the ballside. See Diagram 4-18.

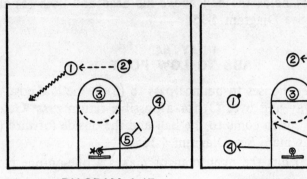

DIAGRAM 4-17                    DIAGRAM 4-18

Player (2) then moves toward the ball and changes direction to cut over the high post man, (3), for a possible lob pass. See Diagram 4-19.

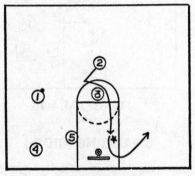

DIAGRAM 4-19

If the lob pass is not made, (2) clears to the offside wing area. Now any of the options (Flex, split, lob to post and corner) is open for (1) to key.

## B. The Weakside Clear

The second way to change sides is for the weakside guard (1) to clear down and around (3). This tells (2) to dribble off (3). See Diagram 4-20.

This may result in a shot for (2), but if it does not, (4) cuts

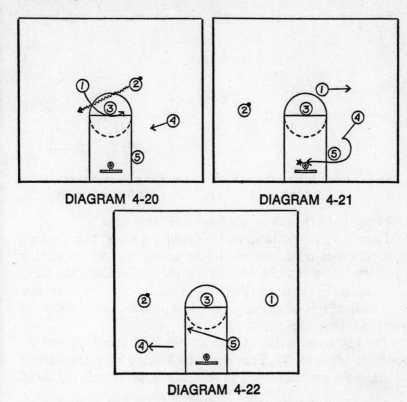

DIAGRAM 4-20          DIAGRAM 4-21

DIAGRAM 4-22

off (5) to the ballside low post and (1) clears to the wing area. See Diagram 4-21.

If no shot is forthcoming, (4) clears to the ballside corner and (5) comes to the ballside low post. The team is in pattern set and may now run the set plays or the Flex pattern. See Diagram 4-22.

## Big Guard Option

If a team has a big guard and wants to post him up in the low-post area, the following option may be run. As (2) dribbles upcourt, post man (5) clears across the lane, (2) then passes to (4) and slashes off (3) to the ballside low-post area. See Diagram 4-23.

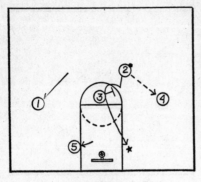 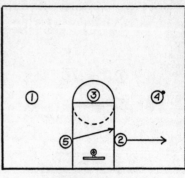

DIAGRAM 4-23              DIAGRAM 4-24

Note that (1) fans to the weakside wing area.

From here (2) posts up and (4) attempts to get him the ball. When (2) clears to the corner, (5) comes across and the team is in pattern set to run the Flex or set plays. See Diagram 4-24.

It must be stressed that the Flex is a very important component of this offensive plan and should be run about every third time down the court.

The key men in this offense are the lead guard (2) and the strongside forward (4). They must be able to read the defense and make the proper play. The scouting report should tell them:

- If (5) can overpower his man, get him the ball.
- If the opposing players are big and slow, run the Flex more often.
- If they are impatient on defense, run the Flex or the change of sides.
- If they have problems on switches, split the post.
- If they are denying the ball to (4), use the dribble entry or backdoor (4)'s man by passing to the low-post man (5).
- If you are behind and time is short, run set plays.

Using the Flex in conjunction with these set plays provides variety and adaptability. It also allows the players to become specialists.

# 5. Combining the Flex and Passing Game Offense

The passing game is the most frequently used offense in today's basketball. As a result, the continuous motion it provides is no longer such a novelty, and teams are better able to defense it. Combining it with the Flex offense provides a new look that could be the winning difference. When presenting this offensive plan to your team, you should point out the following:

A. Both offenses are continuities that require the man with the ball to pass in one direction and then screen away from the ball. The type of screen that must be set is the same and the fundamentals of cutting off and utilizing the screen are similar.

B. Moving offenses do not fight pressure. If you are overplayed and cannot receive a pass, you do not stand still. You go through to the basket, and then get back in the rotation, or you go back and screen for a teammate.

C. The rule of not taking any shot but a layup until five passes are made is also appropriate for both offenses.

D. The Flex and the passing game are both disciplined attacks and the following team principles of operation are vital.

• We do not force the fast break.
• We believe in making the defense work.

- When our offense is disorganized, we bring the ball back out front and start over.

- Because this type of game results in low scores, we must play strong defense.

- Since we take our time on offense and stress good shot selection, teams will attempt to pressure us. We must expect to see a lot of pressing defenses.

- Teams foul most on defense. If we work for good shots, our opponents will commit more fouls than we do.

- Spending a lot of time on defense makes us more tired in the late part of the game. We should be fresher than our opponents at that time.

- Most teams attempt to follow the above principles in the latter part of close games. But when the helter-skelter team with a bad shot selection and a so-so defense forces the fast break and attempts to play in this manner, it is a tough transition. You should point out that since your team uses these principles at all times, it should have a distinct advantage.

## COMBINING THE FLEX WITH
## THE FIVE-MAN PASSING GAME

### Personnel

The five-man passing game is run from a wide one-two-two set. Point man (1) starts at the head of the key with the ball. Wing men (2) and (3) are wide and as high as the free throw line extended. Corner men (4) and (5) are also wide and about as high as the first free throw line blocks. See Diagram 5-1.

When running an orthodox passing game as shown in Diagram 5-2, the man with the ball, (1), passes in one direction and then screens for the first man in the opposite direction, (3), who becomes the cutter.

The five-man passing game has four options for the cutter. This method of combining the passing game and Flex offense allows the point man to come up court and key the passing

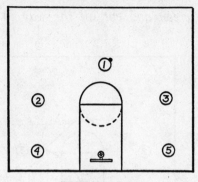

DIAGRAM 5-1

game with any of the first three options or the Flex with a fourth option.

## The Four Cutting Options

The man using the screen, shown in Diagram 5-2, may:

A. *Come to the ball.* See Diagram 5-3.

Note that (1), after screening for (3), rolled to the baseline and replaced (5), who filled the wing position. From there, (2) may also pass and screen opposite and the same options would prevail for the new cutter.

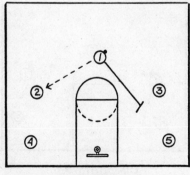

DIAGRAM 5-2

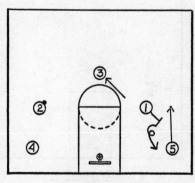

DIAGRAM 5-3

B. *Use the screen and cut all the way to the basket.* See Diagram 5-4.

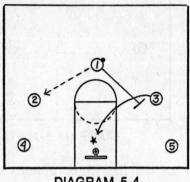

**DIAGRAM 5-4**

Player (1) rolls to the baseline and out to fill the wing. (5) fills the wing and then the point. (3) cuts through and fills the corner vacated by (5) and (1). The rule of motion used to fill the five slots is first in-first out. (Diagrams 5-5 and 5-6.) (2) could pass and screen opposite and the same options would prevail for the new cutter.

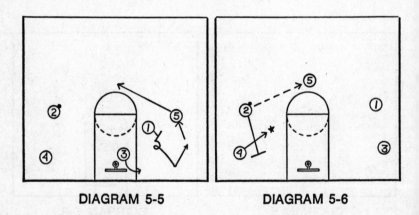

**DIAGRAM 5-5**          **DIAGRAM 5-6**

**C.** *Go behind the screen because his defender is prematurely cheating over it.* See Diagram 5-7.

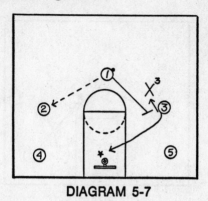

**DIAGRAM 5-7**

The players fill the five open slots on the floor. Player (5) moves first to the wing and then to the point; (1) bounces out to the wing; and (3), after making his cut and not receiving the ball, fills the open corner. See Diagrams 5-8 and 5-9.

From there, (2) could pass and screen opposite and the same options would prevail for the new cutter.

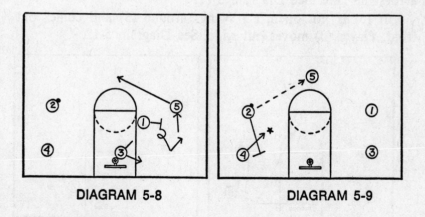

**DIAGRAM 5-8**          **DIAGRAM 5-9**

**D.** *Join (1) to form a double screen for (5), who is coming out of the corner* (Diagram 5-10).

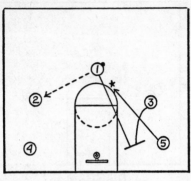

DIAGRAM 5-10

This option is used to key the transition from the orthodox passing game to the Flex offense. It could key either Flex Play #1 or Flex Play #2.

## Flex Play #1

When players (1) and (3) come to screen for (5) in the corner, (5) fakes cutting over the double screen and instead cuts across the lane. See Diagram 5-11.

If (5) is not open, (1) swings around (3) and comes out front. Player (3) moves out wide. See Diagram 5-12.

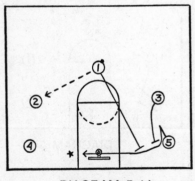

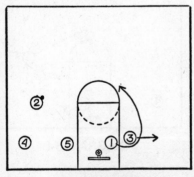

DIAGRAM 5-11                    DIAGRAM 5-12

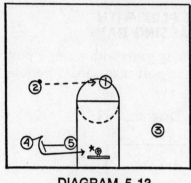

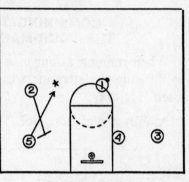

DIAGRAM 5-13                    DIAGRAM 5-14

Player (2) could then pass to (1) and the team would then be in position to run Flex Play #1. See Diagrams 5-13 and 5-14.

### Flex Play #2

This time when (1) and (3) make their double screen for (5), he uses it by coming to the head of the key on the ballside for a possible jump shot. See Diagram 5-15.

Player (3) then cuts over (1) to the ballside post area and (1) moves out wide. See Diagram 5-16.

From there, the team is in position to run either Flex play.

*Note:* Once Option D has been keyed, the team should stay in the Flex pattern.

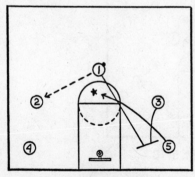

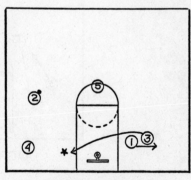

DIAGRAM 5-15                    DIAGRAM 5-16

## COMBINING THE FLEX WITH
## THE FOUR-MAN PASSING GAME

When running a four-man passing game with a single post, it is difficult to determine where the post man should position himself. He may:

**A.** *Play a high post.* See (5) in Diagram 5-17.

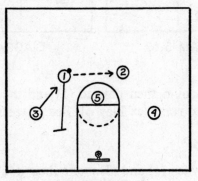

**DIAGRAM 5-17**

**B.** *Play a low post away from the ballside.* See (5) in Diagram 5-18.

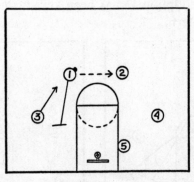

**DIAGRAM 5-18**

C. *Play a low post and come to the ballside only after a teammate has cut between him and the ball.* See (2)'s cut in Diagram 5-19.

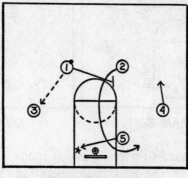

DIAGRAM 5-19

The Flex pattern provides another method of utilizing the post man.

Post man (5) may be used as the key to the transition from the passing game to the Flex. As long as (5) stays in the high-post area or in the offside post position, the passing game would be run. Once post man (5) goes to the ballside low-post area, his teammates attempt to get the ball to him inside or reverse it. See Diagram 5-20.

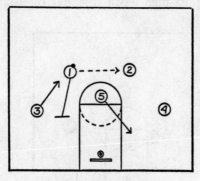

DIAGRAM 5-20

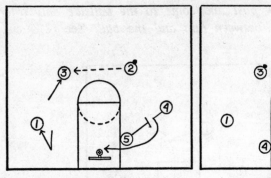 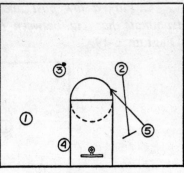

DIAGRAM 5-21                    DIAGRAM 5-22

Once the guard-to-guard pass is made with the post man (5) on the ballside, the Flex is in operation. See Diagrams 5-21 and 5-22.

Once the Flex has been keyed, the team should stay with it until a shot is taken.

## COMBINING THE FLEX WITH
## THE THREE-MAN PASSING GAME

The three-man passing game utilizes movers (1), (2), and (3) and post men (4) and (5), as shown in Diagram 5-23.

The three movers continually pass to, and screen for, each other. The two post men work together by exchanging high and

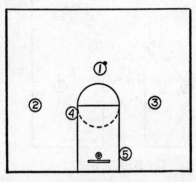

DIAGRAM 5-23

low positions and passing to each other. The result is continuous multi-option motion that restricts players to their areas of expertise. Following are four of the many options that may occur during this motion.

**A.** *Player (1) passes to (2) and screens away for (3). The two post men, (4) and (5), exchange.* See Diagram 5-24.

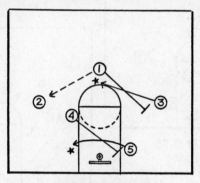

**DIAGRAM 5-24**

**B.** *Player (1) passes to (2) and screens for (3). This time (3) chooses to cut off low-post man (5) and cuts to the ballside layup area.* See Diagram 5-25.

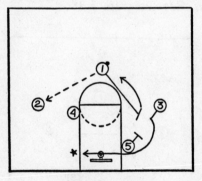

**DIAGRAM 5-25**

Note that (1) moved back to the point to maintain defensive balance.

C. *Player (1) passes to (2) and cuts off high post man (4) to the ballside layup area. If (1) is not open, (2) passes to (3), who has moved to the point (to maintain defensive balance) and screens for (1), who pops out. See Diagrams 5-26 and 5-27.*

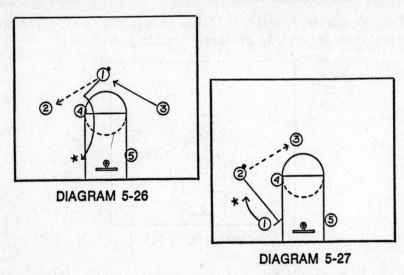

DIAGRAM 5-26

DIAGRAM 5-27

D. *Player (1) passes to (3) and cuts off high post man (4) to the offside layup area. Player (3) may be able to lob to (1); (2) moves to the point. See Diagram 5-28.*

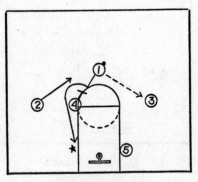

DIAGRAM 5-28

If (1) is not open, (3) passes to (5) and screens for either (2) or (1) (who has looped around (5) and moved toward the ballside corner). In Diagram 5-29, (3) chose to screen for (2). Note that (1), seeing the screen was for (2), backdoored his defender, (3) rolled after screening, and (2) used the screen to move to the ball.

In Diagram 5-30, (3) chose to screen for (1). This told (2) to backdoor his defender, and (1) to move to the ball. Player (3) rolled to the basket after screening for (1).

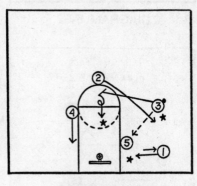
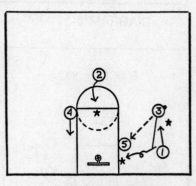

**DIAGRAM 5-29**                **DIAGRAM 5-30**

During this three-man passing game motion, the Flex can be keyed.

## The Flex Key

The Flex pattern can be keyed from the three-man passing game set by the point man (1) in Diagram 5-31. By dribbling toward one side, he keys the offside wing man (2) to dip down toward the baseline and the offside post man (4) to screen for him. Wing (2) then comes out front to receive a pass from (1). See Diagrams 5-31 and 5-32.

From there, either Flex Play #1 by passing to (2), or Flex Play #2 by passing to (3) could be keyed. See Diagrams 5-33 and 5-34.

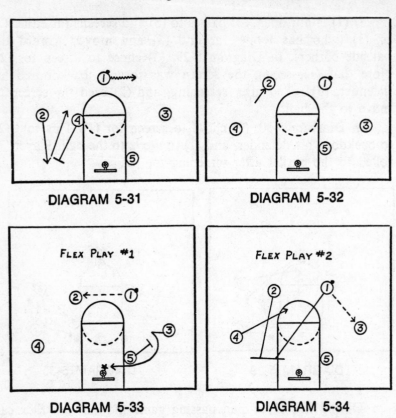

DIAGRAM 5-31

DIAGRAM 5-32

FLEX PLAY #1

DIAGRAM 5-33

FLEX PLAY #2

DIAGRAM 5-34

Combining the Flex plays and the passing game gives a team's offense great variety. It can feature the freedom and spontaneity of the passing game and then quickly switch to the Flex by a simple key. This change provides a more disciplined attack with specific objectives. These two offenses are easily interchanged because they operate within the framework of many similar rules of movement.

# 6. Auxiliary Plays

Auxiliary plays are offensive techniques that may be added as the season progresses that meet special needs, take advantage of the skills of particular players, or simply add depth to the offense. In this chapter, they are categorized as: I. Pattern Set Plays, II. Pressure Relievers, and III. Flex Out of Bounds Plays.

## I. PATTERN SET PLAYS

Pattern set plays are maneuvers that are run so that at their conclusion the team is in position to go into its basic pattern. (The team is in its pattern set.) Following are some pattern set plays.

### The Double Cut Sequence

This sequence has three plays. They are:

*The Guard to Forward Play*

This play is run from a set comprised of high post, (5); two guards, (1) and (2); and two forwards, (3) and (4). See Diagram 6-1.

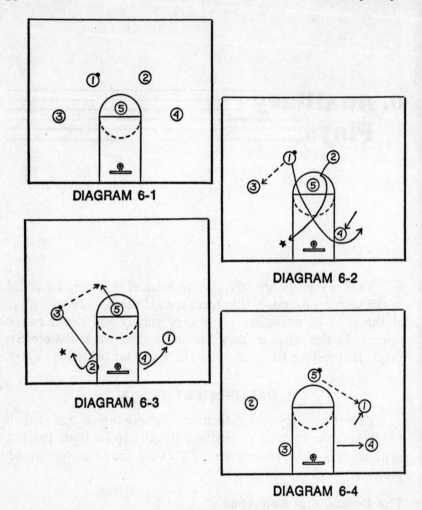

DIAGRAM 6-1

DIAGRAM 6-2

DIAGRAM 6-3

DIAGRAM 6-4

The play begins as (1) passes to (3), cuts through across the lane, and loops around the offside forward (4). At the same time (2) cuts to the ballside post area. See Diagram 6-2.

Post man (5) steps out on the ballside and receives a pass from (3), who then screens down for (2). See Diagram 6-3.

Player (5) may now pass to (1) or (2) moving out toward a high wing position. In Diagram 6-4, he chooses to pass to (1). This tells (4) in the ballside post area to clear to the ballside low wing area.

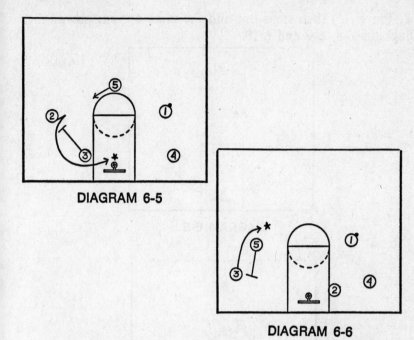

DIAGRAM 6-5

DIAGRAM 6-6

Player (3) steps out and screens for (3) and Flex Pattern #1 is in operation. See Diagrams 6-5 and 6-6.

### The Dribble Entry Play

This time (1) dribbles at (3) and clears him across the lane and around forward (4). Guard (2) again slashes to the ballside post area. See Diagram 6-7.

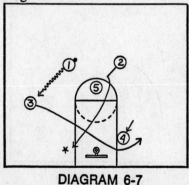

DIAGRAM 6-7

Player (5) then steps out and the same options prevail. See Diagrams 6-8, 6-9 and 6-10.

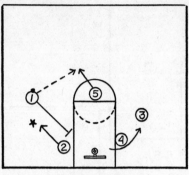

DIAGRAM 6-8

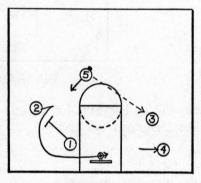

DIAGRAM 6-9

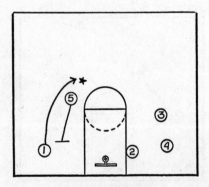

DIAGRAM 6-10

### The Pass to Post Play

The third play of the double cut sequence is keyed with a pass to post man (5). When this occurs, passer (1) cuts down and around offside forward (4), and guard (2) slashes off the post man. Player (5) pivots to face the basket in the event (2) gets open. See Diagram 6-11.

From there, (4) clears and the same options are available. See Diagram 6-12.

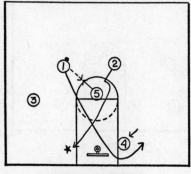
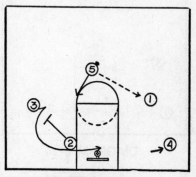

DIAGRAM 6-11          DIAGRAM 6-12

## Outside Cut Plays

The following outside cut plays can lead into the Flex:

### Outside Cut Forward Fake Play #1

Player (1) passes to (3) and makes his outside cut, but continues to the corner after not getting a return pass from (3). See Diagram 6-13.

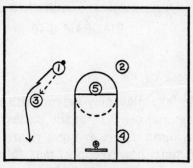

DIAGRAM 6-13

Player (2) then cuts over post man (5). If he does not get a pass from (3), he swings across the lane to screen for (4), who moves to the ballside post area. See Diagram 6-14.

Post man (5) screens down for (2), who loops back to the head of the key. Player (3) can then pass to (2) and initiate Flex Pattern #1. See Diagrams 6-15 and 6-16.

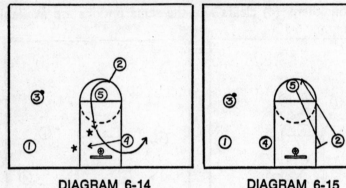

DIAGRAM 6-14                    DIAGRAM 6-15

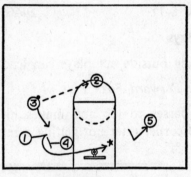

DIAGRAM 6-16

*Outside Fake Play #2*

The outside fake play may be run with a backdoor option in the following manner: (1) again passes to (3), makes an outside cut and, upon not receiving a return pass, continues to the corner. This time, however, post man (5) drops to a ballside low-post position. See Diagram 6-17.

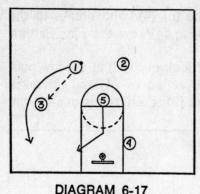

DIAGRAM 6-17

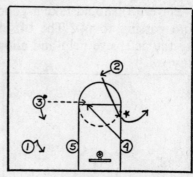

DIAGRAM 6-18

The play continues as offside forward (4) then breaks up and receives a pass from (3). Player (2) takes two steps toward (3) and backdoors his defender. See Diagram 6-18.

If (2) is not open, he clears to the weakside corner. Guard (1) cuts off (5) and the Flex Pattern #1 has begun.

*Outside Fake Play #3*

This variation is functional for a team with a guard, (2), who is a strong player in the low-post area. Player (1) again makes the outside cut and does not get the return pass from (3). Guard (2) slashes off post man (5) to the ballside low-post area. See Diagram 6-19.

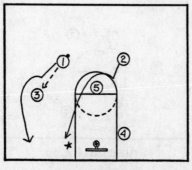

DIAGRAM 6-19

Post man (5) screens opposite for (4), who breaks to the high-post area. The pass from (3) to (4) keys the Flex Pattern #1. See Diagrams 6-20 and 6-21.

Player (3) should take a good look in to (2) at the low post before passing to (4). The offside action by (4) and (5) takes away the defensive help and allows (2) to utilize his one-on-one ability.

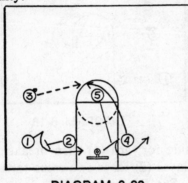

**DIAGRAM 6-20**

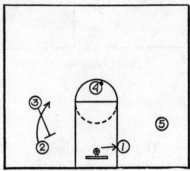

**DIAGRAM 6-21**

### The Guard to Guard Lob Play

In this play, (1) passes to (2) to key the play. Post man (5) steps up and sets a definite screen on (1)'s defender. Guard (1) cuts to the basket looking for a lob pass from (2). See Diagram 6-22.

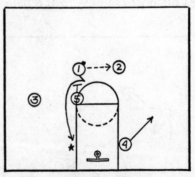

**DIAGRAM 6-22**

If (1) is not open, he continues across the lane. Player (5) steps out front and when he receives a pass from (2), the Flex Pattern #1 has started. See Diagrams 6-23 and 6-24.

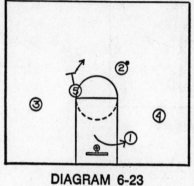

DIAGRAM 6-23

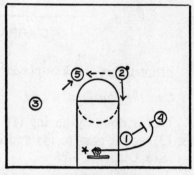

DIAGRAM 6-24

## THE FLEX PLUS THE PORTLAND WHEEL

The Flex may be run in conjunction with the Portland Wheel. Using these two offenses together gives you a strategic edge. If your post man (5) can dominate the area under the basket, the Portland Wheel may be featured. If the defense is strong and more team movement is dictated, you can use the Wheel.

### Pattern Set

Both plays start from the same pattern set maneuver. Guard (1) passes to (3) and makes a slash cut off (5) to the ballside low-post area. At the same time offside forward (4) cuts to the head of the key, offside guard (2) fakes a cut to the basket and then moves to an offside wing position. Post man (5) slides down to a lower post area. See Diagram 6-25.

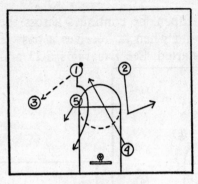

**DIAGRAM 6-25**

From there, the key player is (1). He may:

*Call the Portland Wheel*

This is done by having (1) remain in the post area. Seeing this, (3) would pass to (4) and cut off (5) looking for a return pass. See Diagram 6-26.

Player (5) screens down for (1), who pops out as shown in Diagram 6-27.

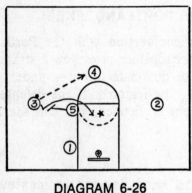

**DIAGRAM 6-26**

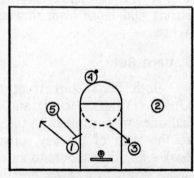

**DIAGRAM 6-27**

Player (4) can then pass to (1) or (2) and screen opposite his pass. In Diagram 6-28, (4) passes to (1) and screens opposite for (2).

In Diagram 6-29, (4) passes to (2) and screens opposite for (1).

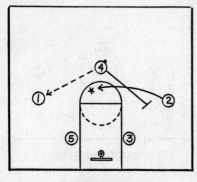

DIAGRAM 6-28

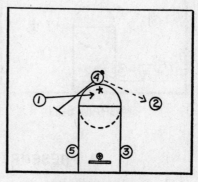

DIAGRAM 6-29

### Call the Flex

Player (1) may call the Flex after his cut off (5) by continuing to the ballside corner. Player (2) again cuts to the offside wing (4) to the head of the key, and post man (5) swings to a low-post position. See Diagram 6-30.

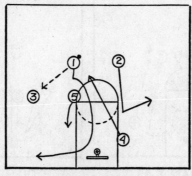

DIAGRAM 6-30

Wing (3) passes to (4) and (1) cuts off (5), who steps out to make a definite screen. See Diagram 6-31.

Player (3) screens down for (5) and the Flex is in operation. See Diagram 6-32.

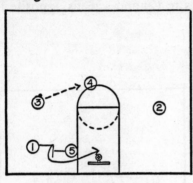

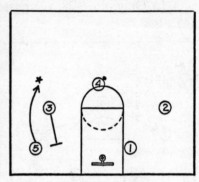

DIAGRAM 6-31                    DIAGRAM 6-32

## II. PRESSURE RELIEVERS

These plays allow a team to play against pressure-help man-to-man defenses.

### Offside Guard-Forward Exchange

In Diagram 6-33, (1) cannot pass to either (2) or (3). It is necessary that (2) be aware that he must screen away for (4).

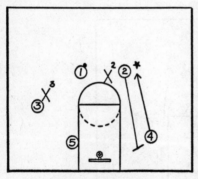

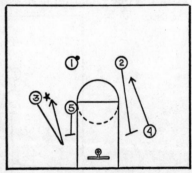

DIAGRAM 6-33                    DIAGRAM 6-34

It also helps if (3) dips down, gets a screen from (5), and then pops out again. See Diagram 6-34.

From there, (1) could pass to (4) and start Flex Pattern #1, or pass to (3) and call Flex Pattern #2.

## Dribble Chase

Player (1) may also use the dribble chase when making a pass that could lead to an interception. In Diagram 6-35, (1) cannot pass to either (2) or (3) so he dribbles at (3) and clears him. In effect, they change positions.

Note that (2) screens away to keep the defense busy. Player (1) could also dribble at (2) and clear him. Note that (3) fills the next slot in the rotation and post man (5) uses (2)'s cut to cross the lane. See Diagrams 6-36 and 6-37.

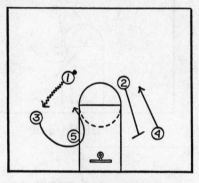

DIAGRAM 6-35

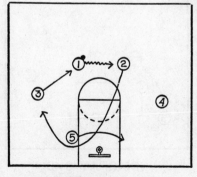

DIAGRAM 6-36

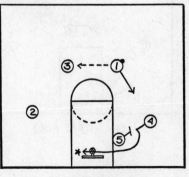

DIAGRAM 6-37

## BACKDOOR PLAY #1
### (Pass to Forward)

This time (2) is being overplayed and cannot receive the pass from (1). Noting this, (4) breaks up and receives a bounce pass from (1). Player (2) then backdoors the overplaying defender (X2). See Diagram 6-38.

If (2) is not open, he clears to the weakside forward area. Forward (3) then cuts off (5) to start Flex Pattern #1. See Diagrams 6-39 and 6-40.

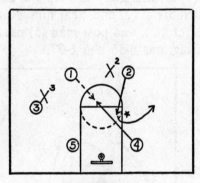

DIAGRAM 6-38

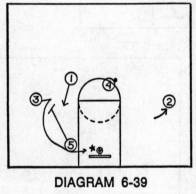

DIAGRAM 6-39

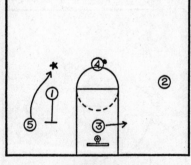

DIAGRAM 6-40

### BACKDOOR PLAY #2
### (Guard Pass to Post)

This time, (5) keys the backdoor play. Seeing that both (3) and (2) are being denied, (5) breaks high and receives a bounce pass from (1). Player (3) backdoors his defender (X3). Note that the offside players (2) and (4) again exchange to keep their defenders busy. See Diagram 6-41.

If (3) is not open, (1) comes down and screens for him and moves out front. Player (5) passes to him, drops low, and the pattern continues. See Diagrams 6-42 and 6-43.

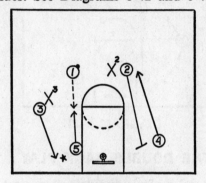

DIAGRAM 6-41

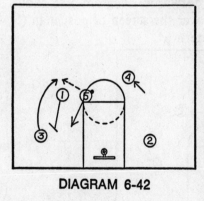

DIAGRAM 6-42

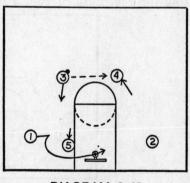

DIAGRAM 6-43

## BACKDOOR PLAY #3 STRAIGHT LOB
### (Guard to Forward)

This play is keyed by the offside forward (4) (Diagram 6-44), who breaks up and calls for the ball. This tells post man (5) to break high and the onside forward (3) to backdoor his overplaying defender. Player (1) lobs to (3).

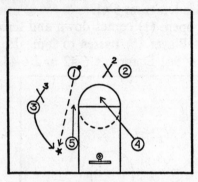

DIAGRAM 6-44

## THE DOUBLE BACK PLAY

One of the theories of playing defense against the Flex is to jam the lane with your defensive forwards. Diagram 6-45 shows defensive forward (X3) cheating over the screen of post man (5) during the execution of Flex Pattern #1.

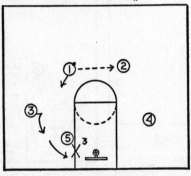

DIAGRAM 6-45

When this defensive technique is being used, (3) should fake his cut and then double back for a lob pass from (2). Post man (5) can facilitate this move by screening (X3) as he attempts to get back to (3). See Diagram 6-46. The result should be an unmolested jump shot for (3).

DIAGRAM 6-46

## THE CHANGE OF CUTS PLAY

This play also may be used when (X3) is cheating over (5)'s screen. Instead of cutting over (5), (3) moves out front, using (1)'s cut as a screen. See Diagram 6-47.

Player (1) then cuts down and around (5) and across the lane. In effect (3) and (5) have changed assignments. See Diagram 6-48.

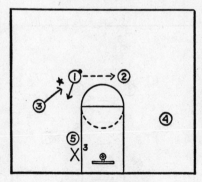

DIAGRAM 6-47

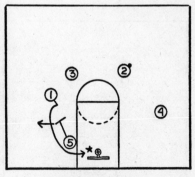

DIAGRAM 6-48

## POST OUT OPTION

At times, when the pressure man-to-man defense is especially effective, the post out option may be used. In Diagram 6-49, (1) has the ball but can pass to neither forward (3) nor guard (2). Seeing this, (3) backdoors and post man (5) moves to replace him.

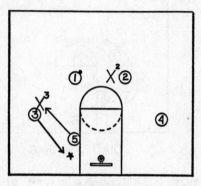

DIAGRAM 6-49

Guard (1) passes to (5) and (4) moves up to screen for (2). Guard (2) cuts to the basket. He may cut inside and look for a bounce pass from (5), as in Diagram 6-50, or cut outside (4)'s screen for a lob pass from (5), as in Diagram 6-51.

If the pass to (2) cannot be made, (2) clears wide and (1)

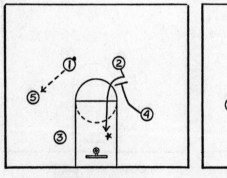

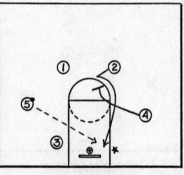

DIAGRAM 6-50                        DIAGRAM 6-51

screens for (4), who moves to the ball to receive a pass from (5). See Diagram 6-52.

From there, either of the two basic Flex plays may be run.

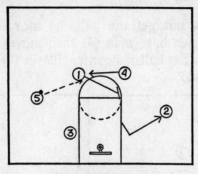

DIAGRAM 6-52

## III. FLEX OUT OF BOUNDS PLAYS

The following out of bounds plays may be run to key the Flex patterns.

### Under the Basket

*Screen the Screener*

The personnel alignment for this play consists of (1) taking the ball out, and a triangle formed by the three strongest inside men — (4), (5) and (3) — and point man (2) at the head of the key. See Diagram 6-53.

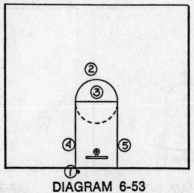

DIAGRAM 6-53

The play begins as the big man on the far side base of the triangle, (5), moves up to screen for the man at the apex, (3). Player (3) uses the screen and cuts to the basket. See Diagram 6-54.

If (3) does not get the ball, he moves out toward the corner. The onside base man (4) then moves up to screen for (5), who cuts to the ballside corner. Player (4) then rolls inside. See Diagram 6-55.

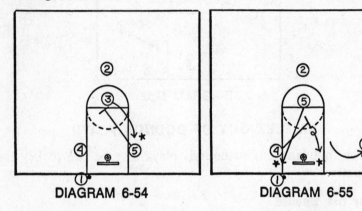

DIAGRAM 6-54                    DIAGRAM 6-55

Player (1) looks first for (3), then for (4) rolling inside. If neither is open, he passes to (5), cutting to the ballside corner. This tells (3) to cut off (4). See Diagram 6-56.

Player (1) then goes opposite his pass and around (4) and (2), who has come down to help form the double screen. See Diagram 6-57.

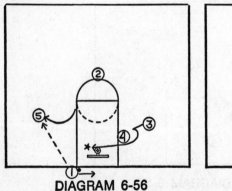
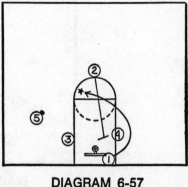

DIAGRAM 6-56                    DIAGRAM 6-57

This is the same motion as Flex Play #2 when run after a weakside guard to forward pass.

If (1) is not open, (2) loops around (4) to the front and (4) moves out wide. From here, either Flex play may be keyed. See Diagrams 6-58 and 6-59.

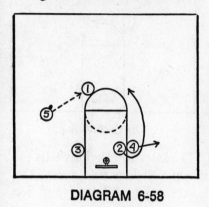

DIAGRAM 6-58

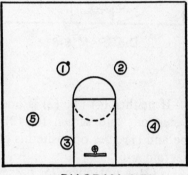

DIAGRAM 6-59

## Box Formation (Screen Up)

This play begins as the ballside base man (5) backs out to the corner. The offside base man (4) then moves up and screens for the man stationed free throw line high on offside (2). Player (2) can cut to the basket in either direction and (4) will roll opposite him. See Diagram 6-60.

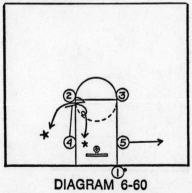

DIAGRAM 6-60

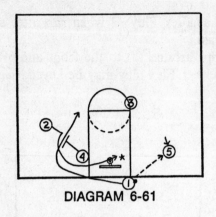

DIAGRAM 6-61

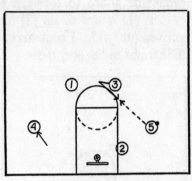

DIAGRAM 6-62

If neither (4) nor (2) is open, (1) passes to (5). This tells (4) to step out and screen for (2). Player (2) then cuts across the lane and (1) goes opposite his pass, around 4, and out front. See Diagram 6-61.

If (2) is not open, (5) passes to (3) and either Flex play may be run. See Diagram 6-62.

### Box Formation (Screen Across)

This time, onside base man (5) chooses to move across the lane and screen for (4). Player (4) moves to the ball and (5) rolls inside. At the same time, (2) moves across the lane and screens for (3), who cuts to the offside corner. See Diagram 6-63.

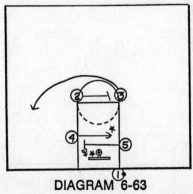

DIAGRAM 6-63

If (4), (5), or (3) is not open, (2) steps out and back and receives a pass from (1). Player (3) then cuts off (5) to the ballside low-post area. See Diagram 6-64.

Then (1) goes opposite the ball and around (5) to go out front. See Diagram 6-65.

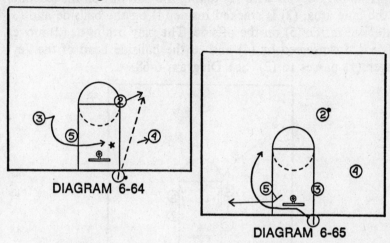

DIAGRAM 6-64

DIAGRAM 6-65

From there, either basic Flex option may be run. See Diagrams 6-66 and 6-67.

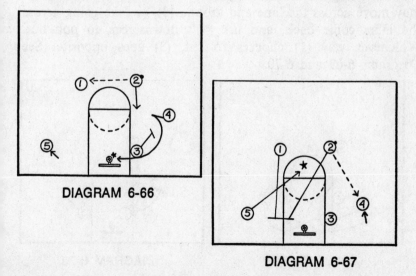

DIAGRAM 6-66

DIAGRAM 6-67

## B. SIDELINE OUT OF BOUNDS PLAYS

### Guard Choice to Flex

This play begins with (1) taking the ball out on the sideline. In the lane area, (2) is stacked inside (4) on the ballside and (3) is stacked inside (5) on the offside. The play begins as (2) moves inside a downscreen by (4) and to the ballside head of the key. Player (1) passes to (2). See Diagram 6-68.

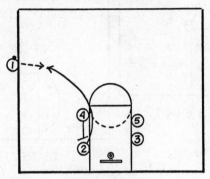

DIAGRAM 6-68

Following his inbounds pass, (1) cuts down to the lane and may move across the lane and around (3); or fake going across the lane, come back, and use (4)'s downscreen to pop out. Whichever way (1) chooses to cut, (3) goes opposite. See Diagrams 6-69 and 6-70.

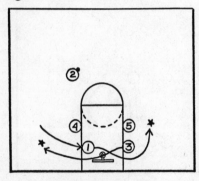

DIAGRAM 6-69

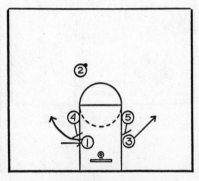

DIAGRAM 6-70

From the double stack, the team can easily move to Flex Pattern #1. See Diagrams 6-71 and 6-72.

The key move is the ballside post man (5)'s cut to the corner to clear the post area.

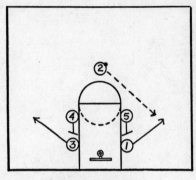 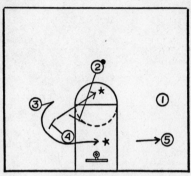

**DIAGRAM 6-71**          **DIAGRAM 6-72**

# 7. Preparing for Zone Defenses with a Four-Step Plan

Teams using the Flex offense can expect to face an inordinate number of zone defenses during any given season. The Flex takes away much of the man-to-man team's overplay on the ballside and practically eliminates the defensive help on the offside. As a result, many opponents will decide to test your zone play.

During my tenure at Eastern Montana College, we had great success against zone defenses. This ability to defeat zone defenses is based on a four-step approach. First, we stressed the fundamentals of individual zone offense; second, we used the same uncomplicated zone movement against all zones; third, we adapted our man-to-man movement as a secondary zone offense; and, fourth, knowing that offensive zone games will bog down, we sharpened our tempo-changing techniques.

## STEP ONE

### Stress the Fundamentals of Individual Zone Offense

Make each of your players aware that:

1. It is easier to fast break against zone defenses.
2. If you play in the spaces between the zone defenders, it confuses them as to their areas of responsibility.

3. You should move the ball at a planned, functional tempo.

4. You must make fake with the ball and, when possible, dribble between the zone men.

5. It helps to throw crosscourt passes.

6. Your player should receive the ball in an all-purpose position that will allow him to quickly pass, shoot or dribble.

7. The two weakest points of coverage in most zone defenses are the high post and the corners.

8. Always go second side. Never initiate the movement on one side and shoot without reversing it to the opposite side (unless the shot is a layup).

9. It helps to study the movement of the defender in your area and take what he gives you. If, when you receive the ball, he is late getting to you, expect to take your outside shot. If he comes at you hard and is out of control, dribble inside the zone.

10. If you are double-teamed, use the two-hand overhead pass.

11. You must charge the boards very hard when you shoot. Part of a zone plan is to give the opponents a rushed outside shot and no second shot.

12. The players are expected to shoot fifty zone shots each night in practice.

13. If you find their zone results in a mismatch (especially inside), take advantage of it.

14. Know the zone game plan for the season and follow it.

15. Know the specific game zone plan and follow it.

## STEP TWO

### Have an Uncomplicated Zone Offense

Rather than describe a wide variety of zone offenses, I will use, as an example, the zone movement we used.

The play begins with two guards, (1) and (2), who play as wide as the lane and about two steps above the head of the key; two forwards (3) and (4), who play wide and as high as the free throw

line extended; and post man, (5), who plays in the low-post area.
See Diagram 7-1.

Once the ball is passed to a forward, (3) in Diagram 7-2, the
bigger of the two guards (2) cuts through to the low-post area
opposite post man (5).

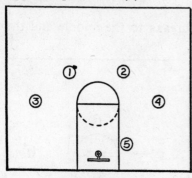

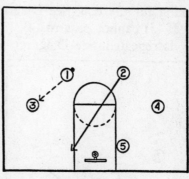

| DIAGRAM 7-1 | DIAGRAM 7-2 |
|:---:|:---:|

This movement declares that (1) is now the back man. It also
changes the offense from an even front to an odd front. This is
important because an adjusting zone would have matched the
initial even front and at this point would be forced to make an
adjustment.

As soon as (2) arrived at the low-post area, the offside
forward (4) breaks to the high-post area for "the triangle play." If
(3) can pass to (4), there is a strong chance either (2) or (5) will be
open for a pass and a power layup shot. See Diagram 7-3.

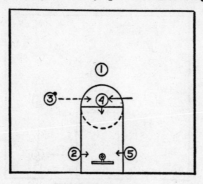

DIAGRAM 7-3

This is particularly true if (4) turns and faces the basket and forces the middle man of the zone to come up to cover him.

If (3) cannot pass to (4), he passes to (1) at the point. This tells (5) to break diagonally up to the free throw line extended and wide. When (1) passes to (5), it tells (4) to cut to the basket looking for the ball. See Diagram 7-4.

If (5) cannot pass to (4), (3) breaks to the middle and the play is repeated. See Diagram 7-5.

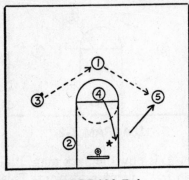

DIAGRAM 7-4          DIAGRAM 7-5

The only variation we used to this simple movement was the UCLA option. It occurs (using the players as they are stationed in Diagram 7-5) when the ballside post man (4) breaks one-half way to the corner. Wing man (5) passes to him. This tells high post man (3) to cut to the basket looking for a pass from (4). See Diagram 7-6.

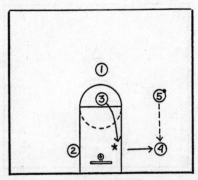

DIAGRAM 7-6

If (3) is not open, (4) passes to (5) and moves back inside. Then (3) loops around (2) (the man in the offside post area) and the ball is reversed to him by way of (1). See Diagram 7-7.

As soon as (1) passes to (3), (5) cuts to the high-post area and the basic movement is resumed. See Diagram 7-8.

This simple offense challenges the middle of the zone. The defense becomes very conscious of covering this area and perimeter shots open up. The UCLA option challenges the short corner and adds variety to the basic movement.

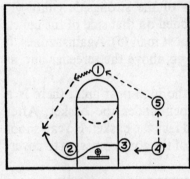

DIAGRAM 7-7

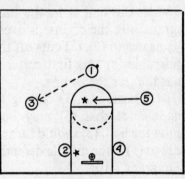

DIAGRAM 7-8

## STEP THREE

### Adapt the Flex to Face Zone Defenses

The above offense served us well, but there were times (as with any play) when things did not go our way. To take care of these occasions, we adapted some of our man-to-man plays to use against zones. We studied our offense to determine which phases had zone potential and then made them part of our zone practice schedule. This additional zone offense allowed us to shift gears when our basic zone motion was faltering. There were times when the man-to-man plays we adapted worked. However, their primary function was to give the defense something different to look at and adjust to. Then when we returned to our basic zone offense, things usually went our way.

Following are some of the man-to-man plays that have been mentioned previously in this book and how they can be adapted to be used against zones.

## FLEX PLAY #1

The basic Flex Play #1 may be run against zone defenses. It provides a method of changing the overload and also tests the middle of the zone.

When the ball is in the hands of the strongside guard (1) (Diagram 7-9), the offense is overloaded on that side of the court. As (1) passes to (2), (3) cuts off the post man (5). Against zones, it is preferable for this first cutter to go above the screener and as high as the free throw line.

If (2) passes to (3) cutting to the high-post area, there is a strong chance that (5) may be open under the basket. After catching the ball, (3) should turn and face the basket. He can shoot or pass to (5) if the middle defender of the zone comes up to cover. See Diagram 7-10.

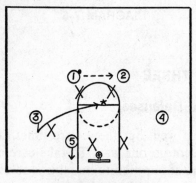
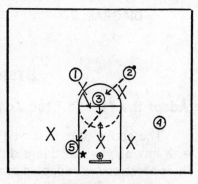

DIAGRAM 7-9                    DIAGRAM 7-10

If (2) does not pass to (3) in the middle, (1) screens down and pins the offside zone players. This allows (5) to move out for a possible jump shot. See Diagram 7-11.

Then (1) rolls wide and the same movement may be repeated. (*Note:* Flex Play #2 is not a strong zone play.)

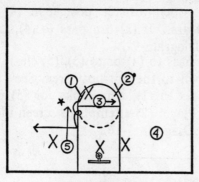

DIAGRAM 7-11

## DOUBLE STACK (Three-Man Motion)

As mentioned earlier, the double stack three-man motion is a strong zone attack.

The three-man motion begins from the 1-2-2 stack formation as both (2) and (3) pop out from the downscreens of their respective post man. This move is difficult for a zone to cover because zone players are taught to play from the inside out and it is possible that they may get caught inside the downscreen on either or both sides. See Diagram 7-12.

In Diagram 7-13, (1) passes to (3) stepping out of (5)'s downscreen. Player (3) looks first for the shot and then inside for (5) posting up.

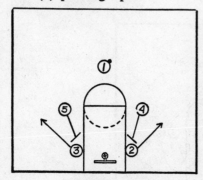

DIAGRAM 7-12

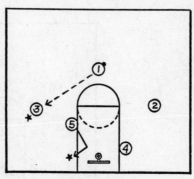

DIAGRAM 7-13

If neither is open, offside post man (4) breaks to the ballside high-post area. If (3) can pass to (4), (5) may be open underneath. See Diagram 7-14.

If (3) cannot pass to (4) or to (5), (5) clears across the lane and (4) slides down to the low-post area. See Diagram 7-15.

Then (3) passes to (1), who looks for (5) popping out of (2)'s downscreen. Player (2) attempts to screen the first defender on that side. See Diagram 7-16.

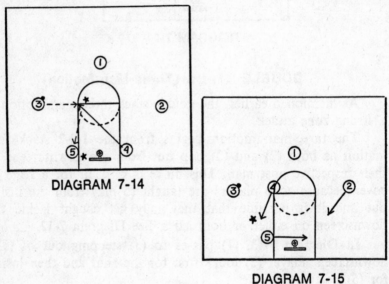

DIAGRAM 7-14

DIAGRAM 7-15

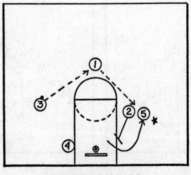

DIAGRAM 7-16

From there, the three-man stack motion may be repeated. See Diagrams 7-17 through 7-19.

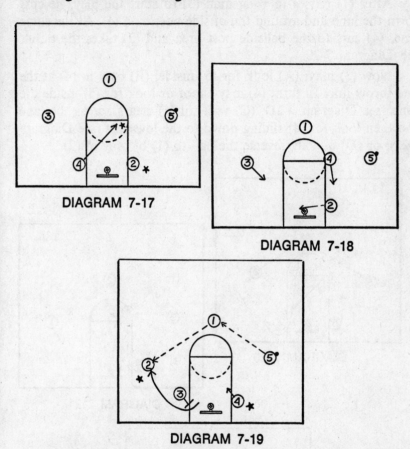

DIAGRAM 7-17

DIAGRAM 7-18

DIAGRAM 7-19

It is also possible to design zone plays that are similar to your man-to-man movement to allow for easy learning by your team. Following are two examples.

## PLAY #1
## THE GUARD THROUGH THREE-MAN MOTION

A play very similar to the three-man stack motion may be run that keeps both big men inside.

## Guard Through Overshift

After (1) passes to wing man (3) to start the play, he cuts down the lane and around the offside post man (4). At the same time, (4) cuts to the ballside post area and (2) takes the point. See Diagram 7-20.

Now (3) may: (A) look for (5) inside; (B) pass to (4) at the free throw line. In turn, (4) may shoot or look for (5) inside the zone (see Diagram 7-21); (C) wait till (5) clears across the lane and then look for (4) sliding down to the low post (see Diagram 7-22); or (D) quickly reverse the ball to (1) by way of (2).

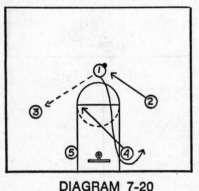

DIAGRAM 7-20

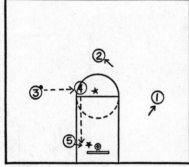

DIAGRAM 7-21

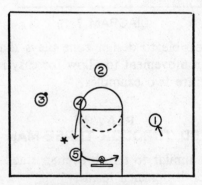

DIAGRAM 7-22

When this happens, it keys the same motion to be run again. See Diagrams 7-23, 7-24, and 7-25.

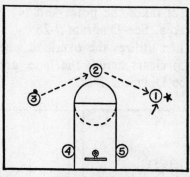

**DIAGRAM 7-23**

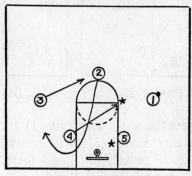

**DIAGRAM 7-24**

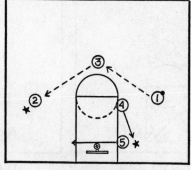

**DIAGRAM 7-25**

## Guard Through Overload

When point man (1) passes to wing man (3), he again cuts through; this time, however, he moves to the ballside corner. At the same time, (2) takes the point and (4) cuts to the ballside free throw line area. See Diagram 7-26.

Player (3) then utilizes the overload when he passes to (1) in the corner, (5) clears across the lane, and (1) looks for (4) sliding down. See Diagram 7-27.

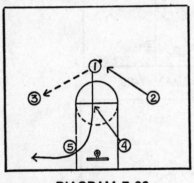

DIAGRAM 7-26

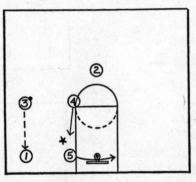

DIAGRAM 7-27

After (3) gets the ball back from (1) and passes to (2), the overload is canceled. Player (3) cuts through to the offside wing and (1) moves up to replace (3). From there, either option may be run. See Diagrams 7-28, 7-29, and 7-30.

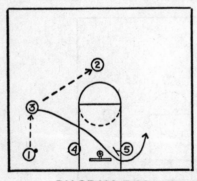

DIAGRAM 7-28

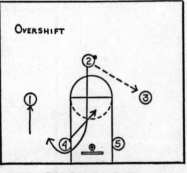

DIAGRAM 7-29

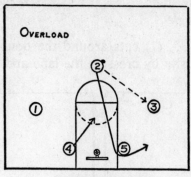

DIAGRAM 7-30

## PLAY #2
## THE GUARD CHOICE PLAY

This play also works effectively against zone defenses. It begins with (1) passing to (2) and cutting down the lane. Guard (1) may now do one of the following two things:

• He may cut around the double stack formed by (5) and (3). See Diagram 7-31.

• He may cut around (4) on the other side. See Diagram 7-32.

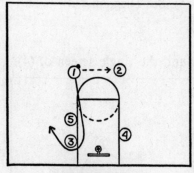

DIAGRAM 7-31

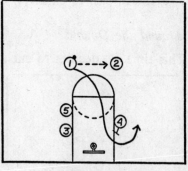

DIAGRAM 7-32

After (1)'s cut, the key player is (3). He always cuts to the opposite side as did (1). The two basic options are as follows.

### Around the Single

In Diagram 7-33, (1) cuts around the double screen. This tells (3) to go opposite by crossing the lane and cutting around (4).

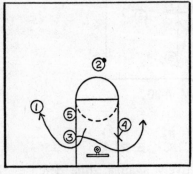

DIAGRAM 7-33          DIAGRAM 7-34

These cuts spread the zone considerably. Since the zone is so spread out, (2) may do the following:

1. He may pass to either player (1) or (3) cutting to the wing areas. It is difficult for the zone to cover both sides at once.
2. He may look inside for (4) or (5). The cuts by (1) and (3) have spread the zone in a way that allow (2) to throw a two-hand overhead pass to either (4) or (5). See Diagram 7-34.

### Around the Double

This time (1) decides to cut around the single screen of (4).

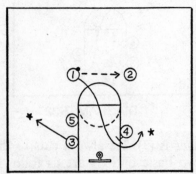
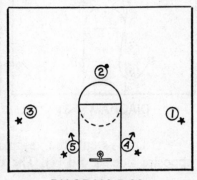

DIAGRAM 7-35          DIAGRAM 7-36

This tells (3) to go opposite him and the same options prevail. See Diagrams 7-35 and 7-36.

From there many things may be done. One good option is to have the offside wing man cut to the high-post area once a pass is made to either wing. See Diagram 7-37.

Then a standard zone play can be run. If (3) passes to (2), (5) or (4) may be open under the basket. See Diagram 7-38.

If (2) is not open, (5) clears to the ballside corner and (1) clears to the far side. See Diagram 7-39.

Then (3) passes to (5) and clears across the lane forming a screen for (4), who moves to the ballside post area. See Diagram 7-40.

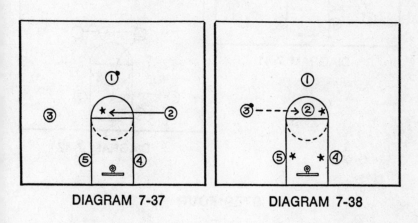

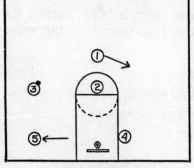

DIAGRAM 7-37

DIAGRAM 7-38

DIAGRAM 7-39

DIAGRAM 7-40

If nothing develops from this, (2) steps out and receives a pass from (5). See Diagram 7-41.

Player (5) would then move to the lane above (4) and the team would be in position to run another guard choice cut. See Diagram 7-42.

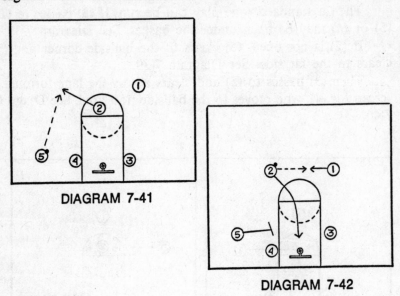

DIAGRAM 7-41

DIAGRAM 7-42

## STEP FOUR

### Sharpen Your Team's Tempo-Changing Techniques

There are times when any given team is "flat" against the zone defense. When this happens to your team, you can speed the game up by:

A. Stressing your running game.

B. Putting on a full-court press, or slowing the game down by:

    1. Holding the ball and pulling the zone out.

    2. Switching to a zone defense.

Whatever you decide to do, the idea is to take control of the game's tempo. Don't go rhythmically down to defeat. Do something different to change the pace of the game.

In summary, I would like to stress that the zone offensive game should not be neglected. Today's zones match, adjust, rotate, fluctuate, and make innumerable other gyrations. This four-phase plan allows you to prepare your players to defeat zones by giving your team:

- individual knowledge and responsibilities;
- a simple function zone offense;
- the ability to utilize man-to-man offense versus zones; and
- when all goes wrong, some tempo-changing team techniques.

# 8. The Disciplined Fast Break

If a team featuring a disciplined Flex pattern chooses to run a fast break, it should be done in a manner that fits its overall offensive plan. The following three fast-break patterns encourage team play and culminate in the Flex pattern.

## FAST-BREAK PATTERN #1

### The Middle Lane Option Pattern

This fast-break pattern has four basic options.

#### The Middle Open Option

In Diagram 8-1, rebounder (4) acquires the rebound, pivots on his outside foot, and passes to outlet man (2), who was the onside front man.

The offside front man (1) cuts to the center and receives a pass from (2). Two lanes are now filled with (1) dribbling in the middle lane and (2) hustling up court in the right lane. See Diagram 8-2.

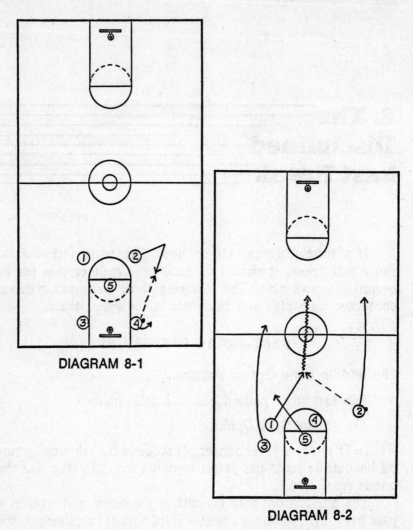

DIAGRAM 8-1

DIAGRAM 8-2

   Forwards (3) and (4) race for the open lane with (3) winning and (4) becoming the trailer. Center (5) is always the safety man and comes down the outlet lane. The guard with the ball, (1), stops at the free throw line and looks for either (2) or (3) cutting to the basket, or for a jump shot. See Diagram 8-3. If these options are not open, (2) and (3) cross by moving through the lane. See Diagram 8-4.

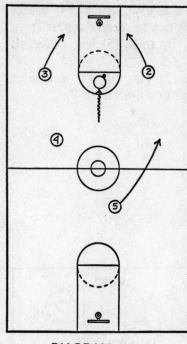

DIAGRAM 8-3

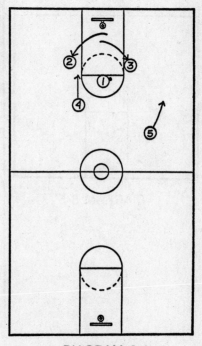

DIAGRAM 8-4

After the initial fast-break wave is over, trailer (4) comes down and screens for (2), who moves out to receive a pass from (1). Player (4) then moves out wide. By then, (5) has moved to free throw line depth. See Diagram 8-5.

As soon as (1) passes to (2), (5) cuts off (3) and Flex Pattern #1 is in operation. See Diagrams 8-6 and 8-7.

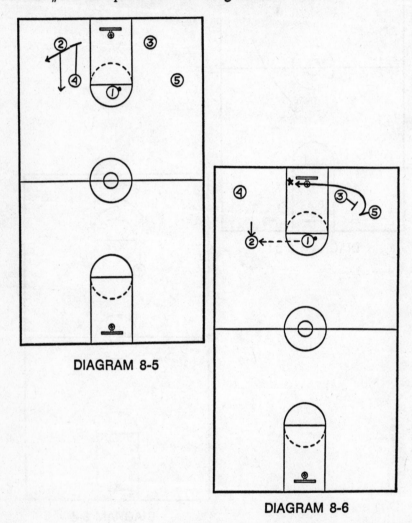

DIAGRAM 8-5

DIAGRAM 8-6

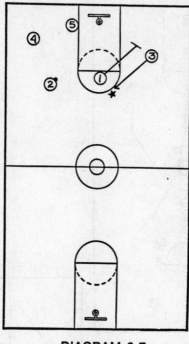

**DIAGRAM 8-7**

### The Middle-Jammed Option

In this option, (2) takes the outlet pass from (4), but cannot make the pass to (1) in the middle. Guard (1) continues his cut diagonally across the court and (2) dribbles to the middle. See Diagram 8-8.

From there, the assignments are the same with (1) and (2) changing jobs. Guard (2) dribbles to the free throw line and looks for (1) and (3) cutting to the basket. See Diagram 8-9.

Players (1) and (3) then cross and trailer (4) screens down for (1). Safety man (5) comes slowly up the outlet lane. See Diagram 8-10.

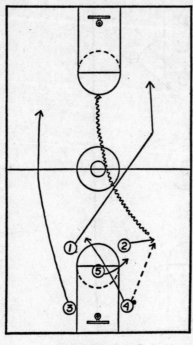

DIAGRAM 8-8

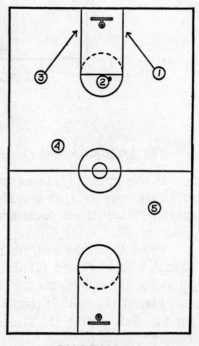

DIAGRAM 8-9

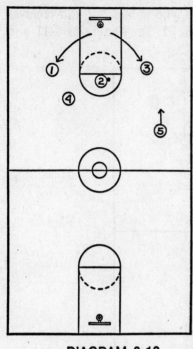

**DIAGRAM 8-10**

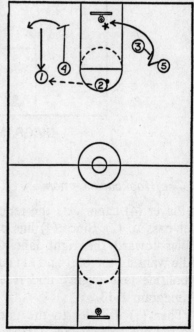

**DIAGRAM 8-11**

Player (4) screens down for (1) who comes out and receives a pass from (2) to key Flex Pattern #1. See Diagrams 8-11 and 8-12.

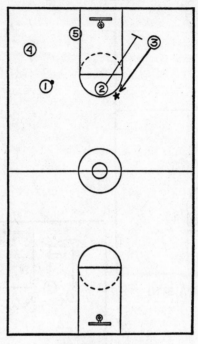

DIAGRAM 8-12

### The Hookback Option

Player (4) again gets the rebound, but he cannot make the outlet pass to (2). Since (4) has pivoted on his outside foot, he dribbles toward the right lane. Then (2) comes back to the middle wanting the ball and (1) cuts to midcourt, hooks back to the ballside lane (right), and receives the outlet pass from (4). See Diagram 8-13.

Then (1) dribbles to the middle, (2) swings wide, and the same options prevail. See Diagrams 8-14 and 8-15.

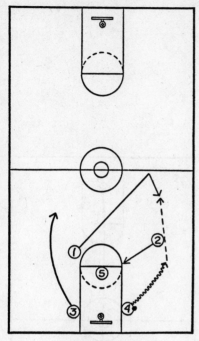

DIAGRAM 8-13

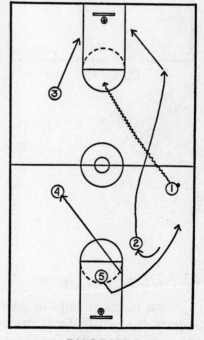

DIAGRAM 8-14

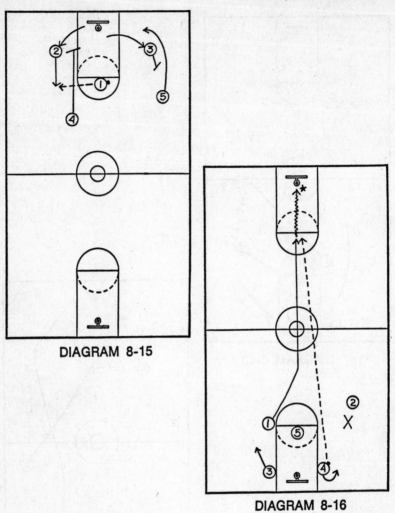

DIAGRAM 8-15

DIAGRAM 8-16

### The Long Pass Option

Some teams attempt to intercept the outlet pass. When this happens, the offside front man, guard (1), may be open for a long pass downcourt. See Diagram 8-16.

## FAST BREAK PATTERN #2

### The Runners' Lane Break

When using this break, onside guard (2) in Diagram 8-17, always cuts to the sideline for the outlet pass. Offside front man (1) runs for the basket in the lane opposite the outlet pass. See Diagram 8-17.

The guard receiving the outlet pass *always* dribbles to the middle. The three inside men, (3), (4), and (5), know they should always run to the outlet lane. In Diagram 8-18 the first one there to fill it is (4); the second, (5), becomes the trailer; the third, (3), is the safety man.

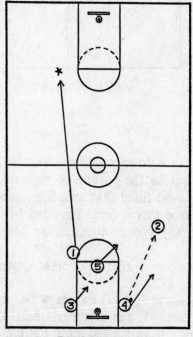

DIAGRAM 8-17

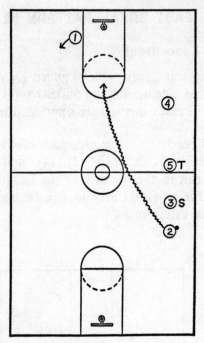

**DIAGRAM 8-18**

Since guard (1) is downcourt first, he cuts to the basket and then "bounces" out to the corner on that side. In the runners lane, forward (4), who filled that lane first, cuts to the basket as (2) stops at the free throw line. Forward (4) clears across the lane and trailer (5) comes through in the same lane. See Diagram 8-19.

If (5) is not open, trailer (3) comes down and screens for him. See Diagram 8-20.

Then (2) passes to (5), (3) swings wide, and (1) cuts off (4) to start Flex Pattern #1. See Diagrams 8-21 and 8-22.

Player (2) may have started Flex Pattern #2 by passing to guard (1). See Diagrams 8-23 and 8-24.

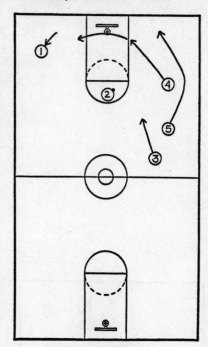

DIAGRAM 8-19

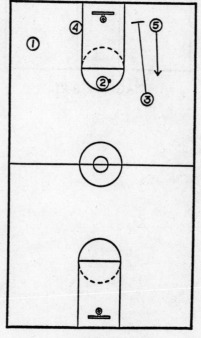

DIAGRAM 8-20

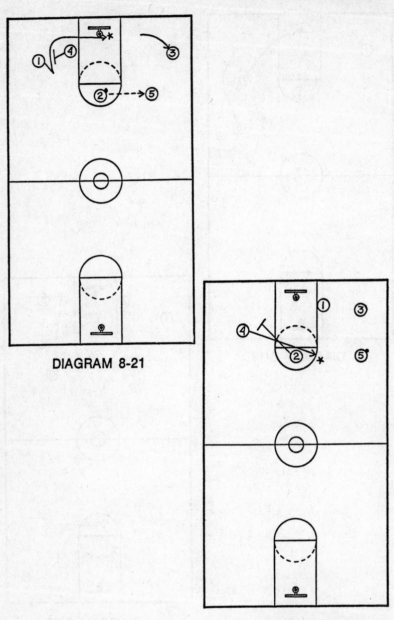

DIAGRAM 8-21

DIAGRAM 8-22

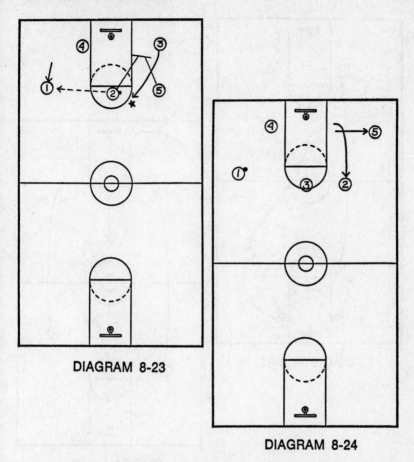

DIAGRAM 8-23

DIAGRAM 8-24

## FAST BREAK PATTERN #3

### The Forwards Run in Their Own Lanes

This pattern is similar to the running lane break, but the forwards (3) and (4) always go downcourt on opposite sides, and (5) is always the safety man.

In Diagram 8-25, (4) makes the outlet pass to (2), who always dribbles to the middle. Player (1) breaks downcourt toward the basket.

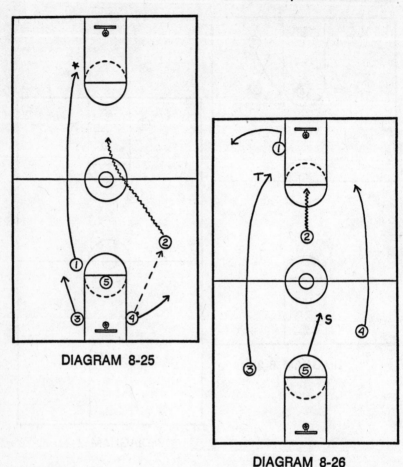

DIAGRAM 8-25

DIAGRAM 8-26

This time, however, forward (4) fills the right lane (on his side of the court) and (3) runs in the left lane. The safety man is (5). See Diagram 8-26.

Notice in Diagram 8-26 that (1), after cutting to the basket, fans to the corner. This move, in effect, makes (3) the trailer in the left lane.

Then (2) stops at the free throw line, (3) and (4) cut to the basket, and cross the lane. See Diagram 8-27.

If neither (3), (4) nor (2) is open, trailer (5) comes down and screens on the side opposite guard (1). In this case, he screens for (3). Player (3) moves out to receive a pass from (2). See Diagram 8-28.

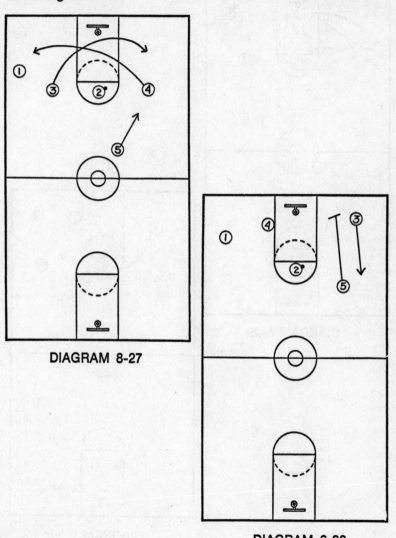

DIAGRAM 8-27

DIAGRAM 8-28

Player (2) passes to (3), (1) cuts off (4), and Flex Pattern #1 is in operation. See Diagrams 8-29 and 8-30.

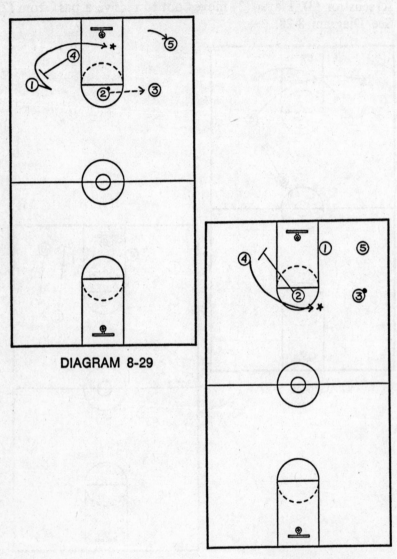

DIAGRAM 8-29

DIAGRAM 8-30

Guard (2) could also have passed to (1) and started Flex Pattern #2. See Diagrams 8-31 and 8-32.

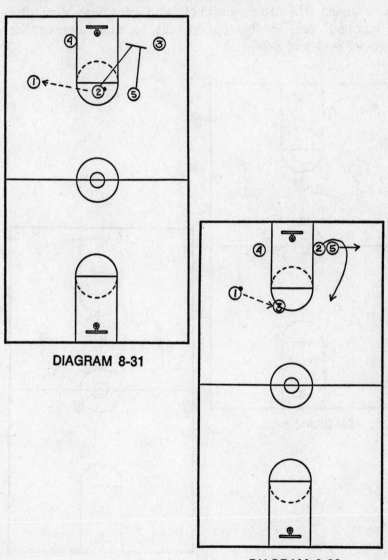

DIAGRAM 8-31

DIAGRAM 8-32

## Special Option

If guards (1) and (2) are great shooters, a special option may be added. The offside guard (1) who went downcourt after the rebound can, in this option, cut to either corner. See Diagrams 8-33 and 8-34.

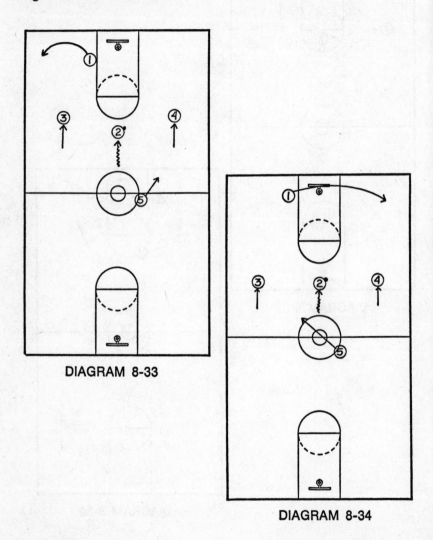

DIAGRAM 8-33

DIAGRAM 8-34

This move by (1) puts extra pressure on the defense, who must get back to the lane to stop the cuts of (3) and (4). This may leave (1) open in the corner. If they worry about the good shooter in the corner, (3) or (4) may be open on their cuts to the basket. The guard with the ball, (2), is instructed to look first for (3) or (4), and then for (1) in the corner. See Diagram 8-35.

The guard-to-guard pass keys Flex Pattern #2. See Diagrams 8-36 and 8-37.

Note that (5) always screens on the side opposite the guard, (1) in Diagram 8-37.

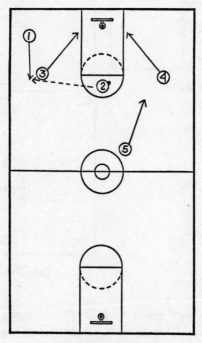

DIAGRAM 8-35

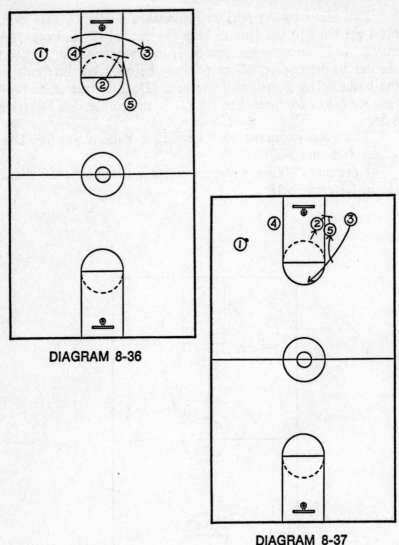

DIAGRAM 8-36

DIAGRAM 8-37

If the pass is not made to (1), (5) still screens on the side opposite (1). Player (3) uses this screen to take a pass from (2) and start Flex Pattern #1. See Diagram 8-38.

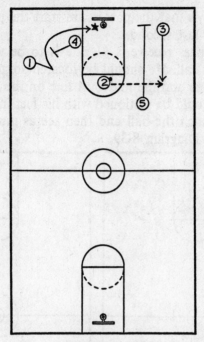

DIAGRAM 8-38

## FAST-BREAK FUNDAMENTALS

Along with running a pattern fast break, if you are interested in playing a disciplined team you should constantly stress the fundamentals of fast-break basketball. They are as follows:

### The Outlet Pass

When a rebounder comes down with the ball, he should pivot on his outside foot and be confident the outlet man will be there. In the past, the baseball pass and the hook pass were considered the best outlet passes. More and more the two-hand overhead pass is being used. This outlet pass can be thrown quickly, accurately, and with enough distance. However, its biggest attribute is that the passer can start the pass and change his mind at the last second.

The outlet pass receiver's #1 rule is to be there every time and call for the ball. He should be located somewhere between the free throw line and the midcourt line on the rebound side of the court. He should be stationed with his feet in a position that allows him to catch the ball and then see as much of the court as possible. See Diagram 8-39.

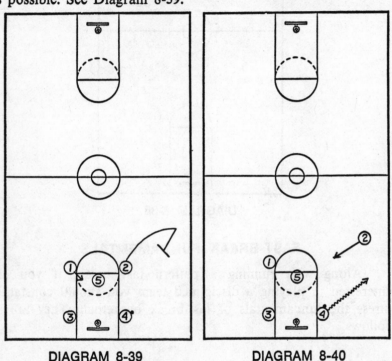

DIAGRAM 8-39                    DIAGRAM 8-40

This makes it easy to immediately see an open teammate and also cuts down his chances of committing a charging foul. When the outlet pass is made, the receiver must "look it into his hands." If it is not made, he should move back to the rebounder calling, "ball." If the pass still cannot be made, the rebounder should dribble carefully up the sideline and expect the outlet man to make his "comeback" move. See Diagram 8-40.

## Centering the Ball

In order to put the most pressure on the defense, the ball should be taken to the center of the court. In the past, most teams have taught the outlet man to pass to an open teammate in the middle lane. See Diagram 8-41.

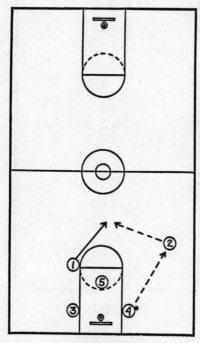

DIAGRAM 8-41

Many teams are simplifying this fast-break component by having the outlet man dribble to the middle. Whichever method is preferred, the ball should be in the middle lane by midcourt.

## Organizing the Lanes

The primary function of the three patterns in this chapter is to offer easy methods of filling the three lanes. The basic problem involved in having a constant three-lane break lies in a judgment call by the outlet pass receiver. Too often he will receive the pass and dribble up the sideline hoping to go all the way to the basket. This closes the third lane to the men attempting to fill it. An example of this mistake is shown in Diagram 8-42.

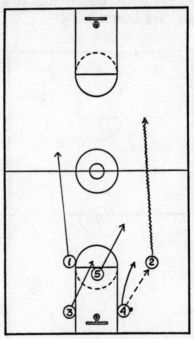

DIAGRAM 8-42

In Diagram 8-42, player (2), after receiving the pass, does not center the ball by passing to (1) or dribbling to the middle. This closes the third lane to (4), (5), and (3), who are hustling to get in on the break. The result is that after the third lane has been closed to the three inside men a few times, they cease to run for it and the chance for a constant three-lane break is greatly diminished. The outlet man should be taught that, after he receives the ball, he must make a vital judgment move. If he can take the ball to the hoop in the outside lane with little or no opposition, he should, of course, do so. But, in most cases, he should expect to get the ball to the middle to open up the third lane for one of his big men. Knowing this lane is open will make the rebounders more apt to look for the outlet man and then hustle for the third lane.

## The Control Area

The exact location of the control area will vary with the abilities of your players and the defensive strength of the opposition. Somewhere between the midcourt line and the offensive free throw line, the lane runners must get under control. If they have really pumped and hustled to fill a lane, they must look up at this point and analyze the situation. The middle man (2) in Diagram 8-43 must change from a speed dribble to a protected dribble. He does this by getting lower and becoming aware of the defenders both in front of and behind

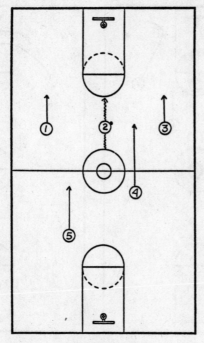

DIAGRAM 8-43

him. He must prepare to stop at the free throw line. The men in the outside lanes, (1) and (3), must make sure they stay wide. They should take one-third of the floor. Trailer (4) must realize that he will be the second wave through, find the proper lane, and be ready to cut at the proper time. Safety man (5) must be aware that he is to be the first one back if the ball is lost, and act accordingly.

## The Scoring Play

At this point, the middle man (2) has stopped at the free throw line and the outside lane men (1) and (3) have begun their diagonal cut at the inside lane blocks. If (1) does not stop at the line, it flattens the offensive triangle and makes the the job easier for the defense. Many players will attempt to split the

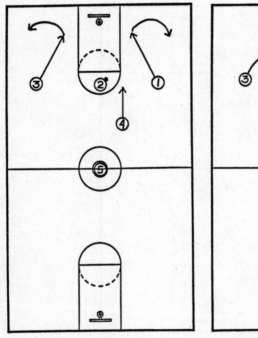

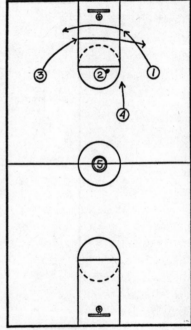

DIAGRAM 8-44                        DIAGRAM 8-45

defenders and then end up with a twisting, turning, jockeying, low percentage shot.

The middle man (2) must make the play. He must be a scoring threat, and then react to the number of defenders and their movement. If it is a three-on-two situation, the jump shot by (2) from the line is acceptable. On a three-on-one situation, the offense should get a layup shot. If it is a three-on-three situation, the type of play depends on your philosophy and the ability of your team. The men in the outside lanes should always be ready to receive the ball. They should be taught to take the ball to the basket, bank it, and expect physical contact. They should plan to make the basket and then make the free throw if fouled.

If (1) and (3) cut through and do not receive the ball, they should wing (see Diagram 8-44) or cross (see Diagram 8-45).

## TRAILER PLAYS

A trailer play is movement by the initial three-man fast-break wave that creates scoring opportunities for the fourth man down. They are usually specific team techniques and are hard to generalize about. However, the following rules of movement are functional.

### Center Trailer Lane

If a team wants to use the center lane for the trailer lane, the middle man must clear.

He may pass and clear way from the ball, as in Diagram 8-46.

Note that the men in the outside lanes, (3) and (1), do not penetrate the lane after their cuts to the blocks. Instead they wing toward the corner and then out to the area of the free throw line extended. This gives the middle trailer room to cut through. Safety man (5) moves into the frontcourt carefully, being sure to protect against the opponent's fast break. He should also be the first man back if his team scores on the break. Some teams are adept at long passing after the opposition has scored on the fast break.

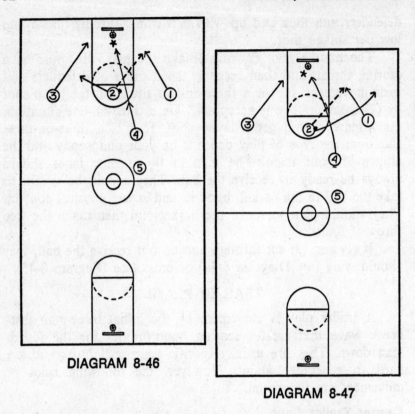

DIAGRAM 8-46

DIAGRAM 8-47

The middle man may also have cleared to the ballside by following his pass for an outside cut. Then (4) has room to trail through. See Diagram 8-47.

## Outside Lane Trailer Play

The key to this type of play is to designate an outside lane to be the trailer lane. In Diagrams 8-48 and 8-49, the outlet lane is the trailer lane. Player (3), who hustled to fill that lane, knows he must clear across the lane if he does not get a pass from (2). This gives trailer (4) room to trail through. Player (5) again stays back for defensive balance.

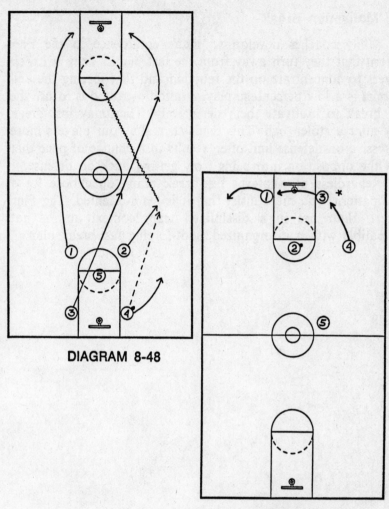

DIAGRAM 8-48

DIAGRAM 8-49

## EARLY OFFENSE

It is wise for a disciplined pattern team, intent on running a fast break, to work on early offense. This tends to prevent bad shots taken when the break should have been over.

## The Motivation Break

Many coaches develop so much confidence in the Flex pattern that they turn away from the fast break. They tell their players to concentrate on the rebound and that forcing the ball upcourt is a low percentage play. A middle ground is to use the fast break to motivate them defensively. They may fast break only after a stolen ball. This tends to make your players more aggressive on defense and often results in a change of pace that lulls the opposition into being slow getting back on defense.

Regardless of whatever fast-break plan you choose for a Flex pattern, you must insist that it is team-oriented. The Flex pattern flourishes in a disciplined team context and is not compatible with a disorganized, shot-forcing fast-break plan.

# 9. Defeating Pressure Defenses

Because of the difficulties involved in defensing the Flex patterns on a normal half-court basis, many teams resort to pressure defenses. The Flex team must be ready to face pressure on many occasions. Following are some ideas that will allow a team to defeat the pressure defenses.

## VERSUS MAN-TO-MAN PRESSURE

Man-to-man pressure defenses have become very sophisticated. They may attempt to: (A) deny your inbounds pass, (B) double-team you, (C) use a switching run and jump plan against you, (D) force you to free-lance or (E) cause you to set up your offense too far from the basket.

### Inbounding the Ball

A team should inbound the ball as quickly as it can after the opposition has scored without causing itself problems. To do this, it must have a plan. One method is to designate a third guard. This should usually be the most agile, best ball-handling forward. After the opposition scores, the designated third guard takes the ball out-of-bounds and the two guards attempt to get open. They may do this by crossing, faking downcourt and coming back, or facing their defenders, pivoting away from them and moving toward the ball. Whichever method they use, the forward should expect to pass the ball to one of the guards as they are moving toward him.

If the guards (1) and (2) lack skills and/or ability, the following play may be run to make it easier to inbound the ball versus full-court man-to-man pressure.

### The Box Formation Entry Play

This box formation play has forward (3) again taking the ball out-of-bounds, but this time the other four players line up in the box alignment in the backcourt. The guards line up on the side of the lane from which the ball will be passed inbounds. The other forward (4) is in the offside layup area and post man (5) is on the offside and almost free throw line high. See Diagram 9-1.

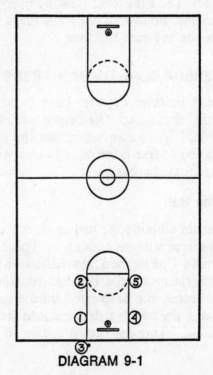

DIAGRAM 9-1

The play begins when post man (5) screens down for (4). Forward (4) uses this screen and streaks downcourt for a possible long pass from (3). Post man (5) then rolls toward midcourt. At the same time, the guard closest to the ball, (1), steps up and screens for guard (2), who is free throw line high. Then (2) breaks to either side and (1) rolls opposite. Forward (3) looks first for (4) and then gets the ball to the open guard. See Diagram 9-2.

Player (5) must keep his eyes on the ball. In the event (1) and (2) are denied the inbound pass, (5) cuts and breaks toward the ball. If (5) receives the ball, both (1) and (2) backdoor. Then (5) passes to the open guard. See Diagram 9-3.

In most cases, however, (3) will inbound the ball to one of the guards (as to (1) in Diagram 9-4). When this happens, (3) goes opposite his pass, around a screen by the other guard, (2), and downcourt.

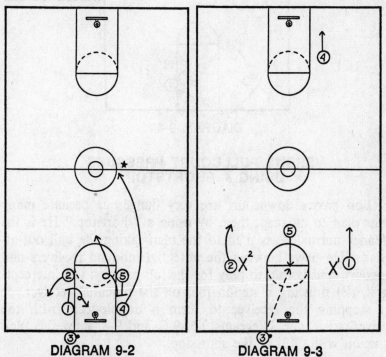

DIAGRAM 9-2          DIAGRAM 9-3

In some cases, (1) may pass to (3), but, generally, guards (1) and (2) must handle most of the man-to-man defensive pressure.

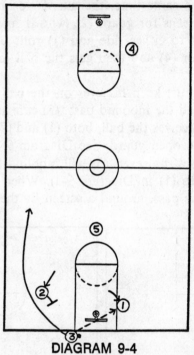

DIAGRAM 9-4

## VERSUS FULLCOURT PRESSURE USING A SHORTSTOP

Lob passes downcourt are very dangerous because many teams plan to intercept them by using a "shortstop." He is the defender normally assigned to the man taking the ball out-of-bounds. He plays between the potential inbound receivers and midcourt, and is told to play for the lob pass by: (A) intercepting it, (B) drawing a step-in foul on the potential receiver, or (C) stopping the receiver to form a double-team with the receiver's defender. Diagrams 9-5, 9-6, and 9-7, show this plan in action with (X3) as the shortstop.

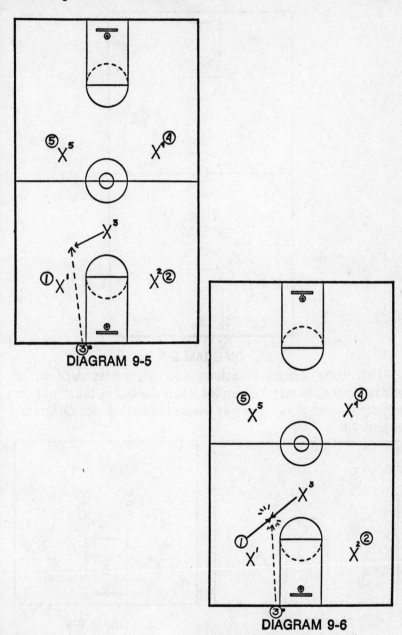

DIAGRAM 9-5

DIAGRAM 9-6

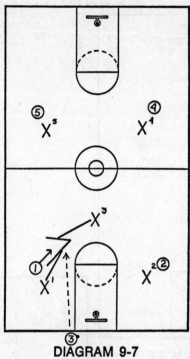

DIAGRAM 9-7

This same defensive technique is sometimes used on a halfcourt basis. It may be applied when the ball is taken out on the side or when it is taken out beside the basket. See Diagrams 9-8 and 9-9.

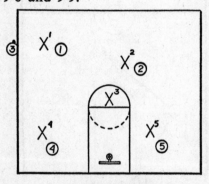

DIAGRAM 9-8

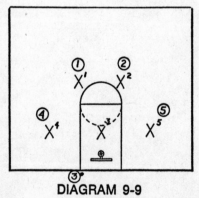

DIAGRAM 9-9

Because of the recent prevalence of this defensive technique, forward (3) should pass the ball to his teammates as they are moving toward him. They must get open.

## Moving Upcourt

Once one of the guards, (1) in Diagram 9-10, has received the ball versus the full-court pressure, the inbounding forward (3) cuts away from the ball, around the offside guard and downcourt.

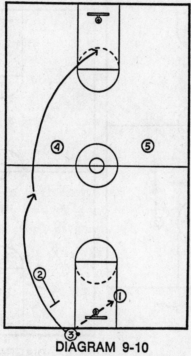

DIAGRAM 9-10

From there it depends on the ability of the offensive guards, (1) and (2). If they are strong and it is a straight man-to-man defense, they should be expected to bring the ball up versus the pressure. They can best do this by knowing what to expect of each other. For instance:

A. The guard with the ball, (1) in Diagram 9-11, should know that guard (2) will, in most cases, stay on line with him as they progress downcourt.

B. Guard (1) should know that if he picks up his dribble, (2) will show up, be open, and move toward him. See Diagram 9-12.

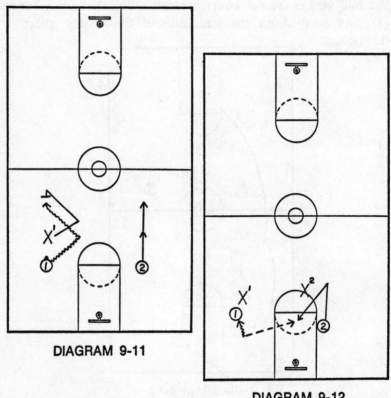

DIAGRAM 9-11

DIAGRAM 9-12

C. Guard (1) should expect (2) to give him the entire width of the floor at times by "looping." In Diagram 9-13, (2) moves downcourt and then loops toward (1)'s side. Player (1) takes advantage of this by dribbling to (2)'s former side and downcourt. Now (2) must be sure to loop back quickly in the event (1) gets into trouble and is forced to pick up his dribble.

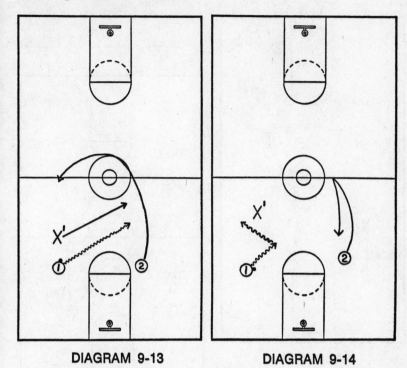

DIAGRAM 9-13          DIAGRAM 9-14

If (2) starts downcourt and (1) does not utilize (2)'s side of the court, (2) must make a V-back and quickly get on line with (1). See Diagram 9-14.

Although the primary responsibility of bringing the ball upcourt belongs to the guards (1) and (2), (5) or (4) can help at times by acting as the safety valve. When either (1) or (2) has been forced to pick up his dribble and the other is being denied the ball by his defender, the offside midcourt man should break to the middle. See (5) in Diagram 9-15.

Guard (1) can then pass to (5) (Diagram 9-16) and a backdoor play can be run. Guard (2) backdoors his defender and (1) makes a change of direction and becomes the second guard through.

Note that (3) clears to the offside in order to give the play room to work.

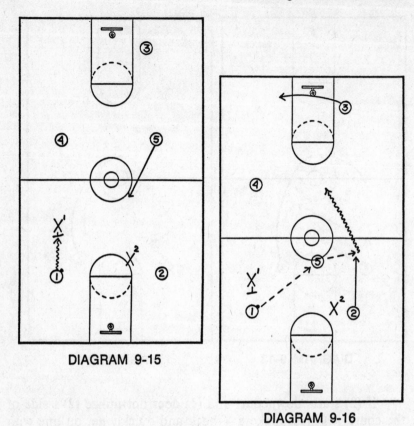

DIAGRAM 9-15

DIAGRAM 9-16

## Versus Midcourt Double-Teams

Many teams double-team the guard with the ball as he dribbles into the frontcourt. They do this with the offside defensive guard ( (X2) in Diagram 9-17). At the same time, they overplay the ballside forward (3) and front the post man (5).

This leaves (1) with what appears to be an easy way out by passing to guard (2). The problem is that the defense anticipates this pass and has the offside defensive forward (X4) attempt to intercept it. See Diagram 9-18.

When (X4) does intercept, the result is an easy basket. To prevent this from happening, the backdoor play again will work.

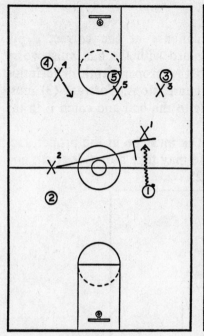

DIAGRAM 9-17

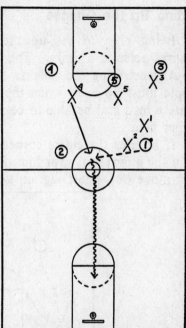

DIAGRAM 9-18

Seeing the double team, (4) breaks to the head of the key, receives a pass from (1) and looks for (2) on his backdoor cut. See Diagrams 9-19 and 9-20.

Player (1) should be taught to throw a two-hand overhead pass when caught in the double team.

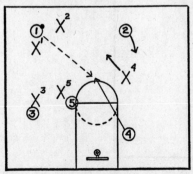

DIAGRAM 9-19

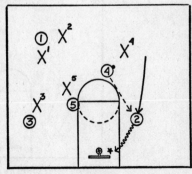

DIAGRAM 9-20

## Setting Up the Offense

Being able to set up the offense at the correct depth requires poise and timing. The guard with the ball must worry about penetrating the defense to the proper depth. The inside people must be open when the guard stops. Forward (3) must create a lead and be able to come to the ball and catch it in the proper area.

If he uses the entire corner, he must be in the proper spot when the guard looks for him. He may fake a backdoor cut and then move out. See Diagram 9-21.

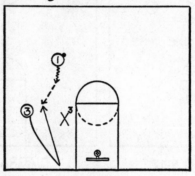

**DIAGRAM 9-21**

Forward (3) may also back (X3) down low, face him and then pivot away toward (1) at the proper time. See Diagram 9-22.

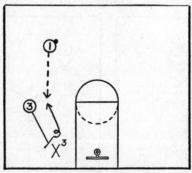

**DIAGRAM 9-22**

Another option is for forward (3) to receive a downscreen from (5) and pop out. See Diagram 9-23.

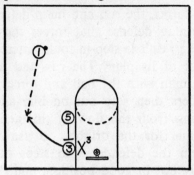

DIAGRAM 9-23

Whichever method (3) chooses, the timing of this cut is all-important. He should expect the pass to come to his outside hand. It is important for (3) to keep his body between his defender and this passing lane and his inside elbow up. There are two proper methods of stopping that (3) may use: One, he may use a jump stop that would permit him to then pivot on either foot. Two, he may use a stride stop, but he must be sure that the inside foot is forward when he receives the ball. This gives him the best protection of the ball as he receives it. This method also gives him the greatest range of motion since it allows him to pivot on his back (outside) foot and face his defender. Many times forwards are called for traveling because they receive the ball with the outside foot forward and then attempt to pivot to face their defender.

The important ideas to remember are the guards must penetrate to the proper depth and the inside men are responsible to time the cut and get open. The tougher the defensive pressure, the more difficult these tasks become, but they also become more important. You cannot allow the defense to dictate your offense by forcing you to free-lance, and/or start the play too far from the basket.

## Facing the Run and Jump
## Man-to-Man Defense

In its lowest terms, the run and jump defense is a constant switching man-to-man defense that forces the offense to play out of control. The result is step-in fouls, interceptions, and the offense forced out of its plan. The run and jump team plays very tight on the man with the ball and forces him to dribble. The other defenders then step out on him and on any other open man resulting from the flow of this action. One simple individual technique for the dribbler to use is to back-pivot dribble away from the defender who steps out on him. The defender is usually not in good position, and this will result in the dribbler being wide open. However, he must be sure not to get out of control because he can expect another defensive player to step out on him. See (1) in Diagrams 9-24 and 9-25.

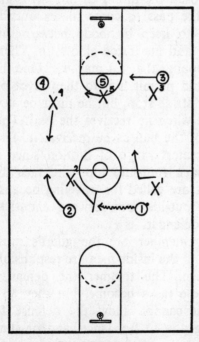

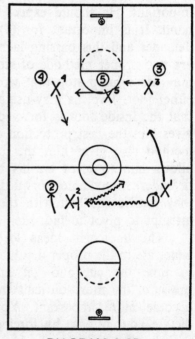

DIAGRAM 9-24                      DIAGRAM 9-25

The backdoor play also works well against the run and jump man-to-man defense. Diagram 9-26 shows it in action. Defender (X2) steps out on dribbler (1). Seeing this, (4) breaks up, receives a pass from (1) and passes off to (2). Player (2) is wide open because it is his defender who steps out on (1).

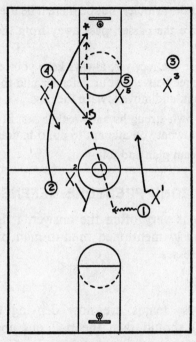

DIAGRAM 9-26

Some general rules to follow when facing man-to-man pressure are:

(1) Be moving toward the ball when you receive a pass.

(2) If you cannot get open, make a V and come back to the ball.

(3) If you are double-teamed, get the ball in the middle and then to the weak side.

(4) Always look downcourt.

(5) Get the ball into the hands of your team's strongest dribbler.

(6) Do not get out of control when dribbling.

(7) The pass across the foul lane in the backcourt can beat you.

(8) Elongate the press by sending someone downcourt.

(9) When you are forced to pick up your dirbble, use the two-hand overhead pass.

(10) Jump balls are better than lost balls. Don't be in a hurry.

(11) Don't crowd the dribbler, but be there if he needs you.

(12) When you are the passer, pass away from the defender and chest high.

(13) When you are the receiver, always keep your eye on the ball, assume a stance between your defender and the ball, give the passer a target, and move toward the pass.

(14) Know your own strengths and weaknesses. Stay within their boundaries in what you attempt to do. If in doubt, don't!

(15) Know you team plan and follow it.

## VERSUS ZONE PRESSURE DEFENSES

Since simplicity is very often the answer, it is wise to use many of the previously mentioned man-to-man press-defeating ideas versus zone presses.

### Inbounding the Ball

Many zone press teams are now denying the inbounds passes. Forward (3) should take the ball out and the guards should attempt to get open.

Once it has been passed to either guard ((1) in Diagram 9-27), (3) should clear around the offside guard (2) and go all the way down the court. This movement elongates the zone press and makes the jobs of the defensive players more difficult.

By then, the offside midcourt man should be in the middle as per the backdoor play. At this time, it should be noted that against zone pressure (1) should dribble only as a last resort. Player (1) should expect to be double-teamed and should have the ball above his head with his elbows out. He should be prepared to throw a two-hand overhead pass. He has three choices: *A.* His first preference is to throw it to (4) in the middle. When this happens (2) makes the same backdoor move even though he probably has no defender on him. Player (4) passes to (2) who may be able to take it upcourt. See Diagram 9-28.

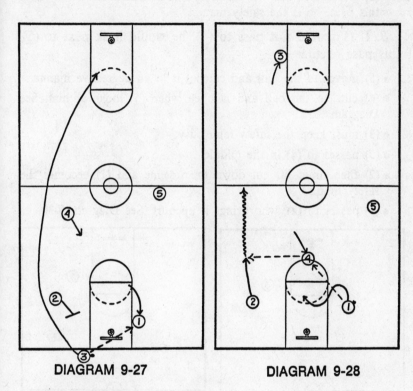

DIAGRAM 9-27          DIAGRAM 9-28

The factors that make this maneuver work are:

- (3) goes downcourt and elongates the pressure because (X5) is forced to cover him.
- All five defenders are on the ballside of the court. This is the case when playing against tough zone pressing teams.
- (5) is at midcourt on the ballside and spreads (X4)'s coverage between himself and (4). This allows (4) to get open in the middle.
- (4) breaks to the middle at the right time and assumes a

functional receiving position. He should catch the pass from (1) as if he were pulling down a rebound.

● (2) times his cut down the weak side and stays wide enough.

● (1) is able to fight off the double-team and pass to (4). After this pass, he is the safety man.

*B.* If (1) could not pass to (4), he would look next to (5). If this pass occurs:

● (5) moves to the ball and catches it in an aggressive manner.

● (4) cuts to the ball and is open when (5) looks at him. See Diagram 9-29.

● (3) must keep the safety man busy.

● (5) passes to (4) in the middle.

● (2) then times his cut down the sideline and (1) becomes the safety man.

● (4) passes to (2), who brings it upcourt. See Diagram 9-30.

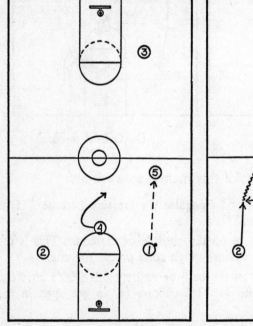

DIAGRAM 9-29

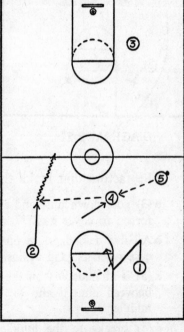

DIAGRAM 9-30

*C.* If (1) can pass to neither (4) in the middle nor (5) on the side, he can pass to (2). He must constantly be reminded that this is a dangerous pass. It is across the backcourt free-throw lane and any interception usually results in an easy basket for the opposition. However, if this pass is completed, it puts a lot of pressure on the zone pressure defense. The defensive team must make very long lateral defensive slides and some of them must switch assignments. Because of the many defensive adjustments this pass makes necessary, it is often easy to get the ball in the middle once this pass is made. To encourage this, (4) moves to the ballside sideline and (5) cuts into the middle. See Diagram 9-31.

Once the pass is made, the same options are available. Player (2) may pass to (5) in the middle (which would key (1)'s backdoor move), to (4) on the side, or back across the lane to (1).

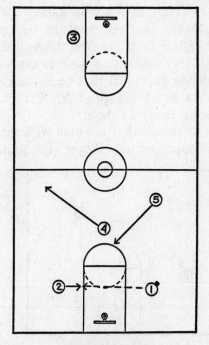

DIAGRAM 9-31

The fact that this zone press pattern is so closely related to the man-to-man press pattern concepts is a distinct advantage. It makes a better teaching situation and also makes it easier to meet and defeat teams that use combination or changing full-court pressure defenses.

## VERSUS HALF-COURT PRESSURE

Although half-court zone pressure defenses are relatively rare, it is wise to have a plan that permits you to combat any double-teaming in the frontcourt. This includes double-teams that develop out of a man-to-man defense.

Any time a defensive team double-teams, an offensive player is open. The idea then is to create enough passing outlets for the man with the ball, insist that the ball is moved around, and as a result get the ball to the open man. This can best be done, as shown in Diagram 9-32, by having the post man (5) stay high and between the ball and the basket; the ballside forward (3) play higher than the free throw line extended; the offside forward (4) stay lower than the free throw line extended; and telling the offside guard (2) that he is usually the one that is open. He should take advantage of this fact by sliding into an open area and being ready to shoot.

These problems ensure that the man with the ball will have plenty of passing opportunities. Player (1) should be told that

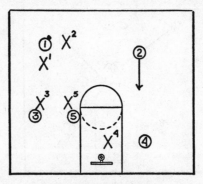

**DIAGRAM 9-32**

his number one option is (5) in the middle. The next option would be to forward (3). Finally, it should be pointed out that although (2) is the third passing option, many teams will double-team the guard with the ball and "shoot" the offside forward to intercept a guard-to-guard pass. See Diagram 9-33.

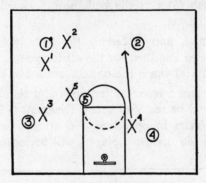

DIAGRAM 9-33

The sure way to get the ball to (2) safely is to relay it by way of post man (5). When this is done, (2) is usually wide open. See Diagram 9-34.

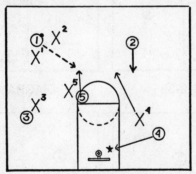

DIAGRAM 9-34

If the ball is passed to (5) and (X4) is "shooting the gap," (4) will be open under the basket.

In general, the rules against a double half-court defense are:

1. The post man must play high.

2. Move the ball.

3. Use the two-hand overhead pass when double-teamed.

4. Get the ball into (5) in the middle as much as possible.

5. The forwards should play up on the ballside and down on the offside. When (5) gets the ball, both forwards should move toward the basket.

6. The post man, upon receiving the ball, looks first for the offside forward and then for the offside guard. He should also be aware that at times the onside forward is open.

7. The offside guard is very often open and should slide into an open area and be ready to shoot. Diagrams 9-35 through 9-40 show these rules in operation. No attempt will be made to show where the defensive players will be located.

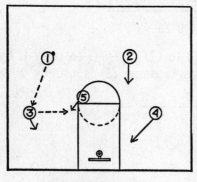

DIAGRAM 9-35

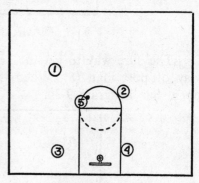

DIAGRAM 9-36

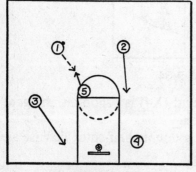

DIAGRAM 9-37

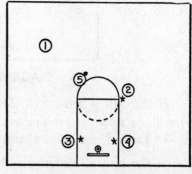

DIAGRAM 9-38

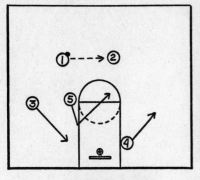

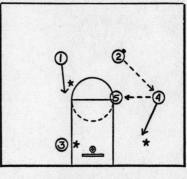

DIAGRAM 9-39                    DIAGRAM 9-40

These rules provide more than just a one-half court press pattern. They offer a method of combatting any attempt at double-teaming.

In summary, it should be repeated that well-disciplined teams featuring the Flex pattern will face more pressure defenses than an average team. Because of this, the pressure game offense must be a basic component of their overall practice plan. The fundamental individual skills and team technique assignments involved must be repeated until the players react immediately and with confidence.

# 10. Analyzing the Flex Pattern

The Flex pattern is a fundamentally sound offense. To prove this statement, you must evaluate it in terms of the fundamentals of man-to-man offense.

A fundamentally sound offense has:

1. A system for maintaining defensive balance.
2. Patterns that provide high percentage shots.
3. A rebounding plan.
4. The proper movement for the personnel involved.
5. An adjustable time factor that offers both quick shots and time-consuming pattern options.
6. Provisions for individual initiative.
7. Play keys that are easy to read.
8. Functional basic play components.
9. Plays that may be adapted to use versus zone defenses.
10. Built-in pressure relief mechanisms.
11. Patterns that are conducive to a team effort.

How does the Flex measure up in regard to these vital criteria?

## MAINTAINING DEFENSIVE BALANCE

Since the Flex pattern is a movement-oriented offense, defensive balance could be a problem. Many coaches feel it is easy to fast-break against continuity offenses and make their plans accordingly. To be ready for this eventuality, you (the Flex coach) may consider these three plans for maintaining defensive balance.

First, you can designate a primary defensive balance man. This is usually a small, quick guard. Some teams call him a "mouse." This player has no offensive rebounding responsibility and is the first man back to the defensive free throw lane once the opposition obtains the ball. There is a problem inherent in this offense where the other guard must cover him. If the "mouse" (see (1) in Diagram 10-1) is the first cutter in Flex Pattern #1 and takes the shot, the other guard, (2), must maintain defensive balance.

Second, you can make both guards be responsible. The guard in a front position stays back when a shot is taken. A player is in a front position if one of his teammates is between him and the basket. If neither guard is in a front position, the one on the side away from the shot is back. Here are some examples. In Diagram 10-2, (2) is back beacuse he is a front man and (1) is inside.

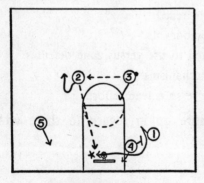

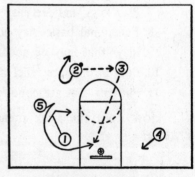

DIAGRAM 10-1                    DIAGRAM 10-2

In Diagram 10-3, (1) is the back man because, even though both he and (2) are front men, at the time of the shot, he (1) is away from the side of the shot.

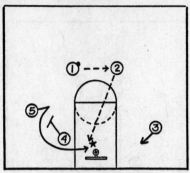

DIAGRAM 10-3

In Diagram 10-4, neither guard is in a front position, but (2) is away and, as a result, is the back man.

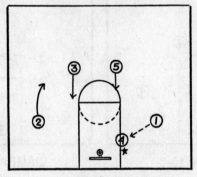

DIAGRAM 10-4

Third, you may use the front and away rule for all five players. The offside front man is always back. (See (5) in Diagram 10-5.) Player (4) shoots and (5) is the front and away man, so he stays back.

Another example would be (2) in Diagrams 10-6 and 10-7. At the culmination of these two diagrams, (3) shoots and (2) is front and away so he stays back.

Whichever method you decide to adopt, you must make it part of the practice plan. You should devote part of each practice week to maintaining defensive balance.

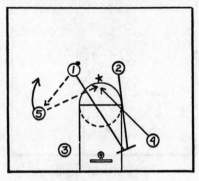

**DIAGRAM 10-5**

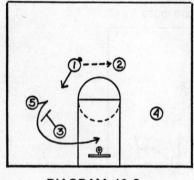

**DIAGRAM 10-6**

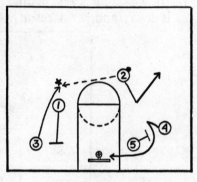

**DIAGRAM 10-7**

## GETTING A HIGH PERCENTAGE SHOT

The movement of this offense causes the defense to Flex. The defense must contract to cover against a potential layup by jamming the lane. Then they must move out (expand) to cover a potential outside shot. This constant defensive approaching and retreating requires excellent defensive footwork and mental discipline. The result is very often mistakes that lead to easy baskets.

The second thing the Flex movement does is to weaken the two basic tools of the pressure-help man-to-man defense. The constant movement engages the weakside (help) defenders. They become preoccupied with fighting through screens and moving with their man. This weakens the help and, as a result, makes the defenders on the ballside weary of overplaying their man.

Along with causing the defense to Flex and destroying their pressure-help plan, the offense is built to be a continuity with high percentage options. The offensive players, through repetition, become very adept at getting open. The shots that result are either layups or unmolested 10- to 12-foot jump shots. The players soon learn that if they are disciplined and patient, the defense will either let up or make a mistake. The resulting shot will be one they have worked on many times.

## THE REBOUNDING PLAN

Part of the rebounding plan is knowing who is responsible for defensive balance. This gives the other players the confidence to "storm" the boards when a shot is taken.

The second phase of the rebounding plan is built into running the Flex continuity. The continuous five-man movement makes it very difficult for defensive men to make a strong blockout when a shot is taken. This is especially true if they lack the ability to open up and see the ball away from the play.

The third factor composing the plan is shot anticipation. The Flex pattern is repetitious. The players can develop the ability to see an option breaking open and to expect a shot to be taken. This gives them a slight advantage over the opposition and may provide a split second to beat the potential blockout. You would be wise to point this fact out to your players and set up practice situations to develop the ability to anticipate this. Taking Flex Pattern #1 as an example, you can safely theorize that if a shot is missed off the first option (see Diagram 10-8),

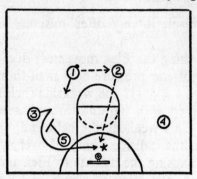

**DIAGRAM 10-8**

it will come down close to the backboard. This requires an
offensive rebounder to fight his way all the way in. However, in
option two of Flex Pattern #1, the shot will be taken on one
side of the lane and probably at least as high as the free throw
line. In that case, an offensive rebounder should fight for a
strongly-based position in front of the basket or on the side
away from the shot. See Diagram 10-9.

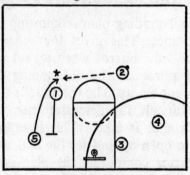

**DIAGRAM 10-9**

Finally, there is the matter of technique. An offensive
rebounder must watch the ball and expect the defender to make
contact. From there, his four jobs are:

A. Get around the blockout. He does this by either stepping over
the defender's leg on the side of the potential rebound, or
spinning off the defender.

   B. Moving to an advantageous area. This may involve establishing an area by cutting off the opposition's path to it, using elbows and/or hips.

   C. Assuming a wide strongly-based position to hold the area the rebounder has claimed.

   D. Going for the rebound in a very authoritative manner.

## UTILIZING PROPER MOVEMENT

Any consideration of movement must include the amount, the tempo, the function, and how it fits the personnel involved.

### Amount of Movement

The Flex is a movement-oriented offense. This fact is one of its basic strengths. Most teams play what could be called a three-pass offense. The forwards and center come upcourt and stand still until the guards bring the ball upcourt. A guard then passes the ball inside and cuts through; usually after two more passes, a shot is taken. This lack of movement makes a defensive player's assignment relatively easy. However, the Flex team may make ten to fifteen passes before a shot is taken. These passes are made in the context of constant movement. This requires a degree of both mental and physical toughness that severely tests most defenses.

Other attributes accrue by making the opposition play a lot of defense. Defense is more tiring than offense. As a result, a team that has practiced primarily against its own three-pass offense and then faces the Flex pattern may show the effects of all the physical movement and mental discipline as the game wears on. This fatigue will usually affect both individual and team offensive performances. Tired players tend to make more mechanical and mental errors. As a team on offense, they will almost predictably tend to change their offense by making more passes and slowing the tempo. They will begin to imitate the Flex team as a subconscious mechanism to keep from playing so much defense. When the opposition plays your game, you are usually in an advantageous position and this is no exception— most fouls are committed on defense. It follows then that since the Flex team makes more passes and has a disciplined approach to shot selection that over a season the opponents will commit many more fouls.

## The Offensive Tempo

Some continuities tend to lose their effectiveness if they are run at a fast tempo. This does not seem to be true with the Flex pattern. It should be run as quickly as the talents of the players will allow. They must be able to execute the fundamentals involved and, at the same time, be aware of each scoring option as it occurs. It is helpful if they can successfully do those things at an up tempo.

## The Pattern's Function

As has been mentioned, this pattern causes the defense to Flex. This constant contracting to cover the inside options and expanding to cover the outside options can lead to mistakes in footwork and judgment. The result is defensive errors that lead to many easy baskets.

Another factor that cannot be overlooked is that the Flex is an interchangeable five-man continuity. That means at various times each offensive player will be a guard, a forward, or a post man. As a result, the opposition's big post man will, at times, be defending a post man. This is asking a lot of the average defender and is a plus for the offense.

## The Personnel Involved

This is an area where you must carefully analyze the Flex as it relates to your team. Point out to your players where the team is strong. For example, in Diagram 10-10, (3) is a very strong player in the post. The team is running Flex Pattern #1. Player (2) must be told that even if (3) does not get open on his cut off (5), it would be wise to take some time and get the ball into him. See Diagram 10-11.

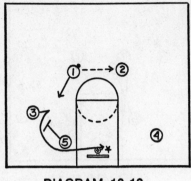

**DIAGRAM 10-10**

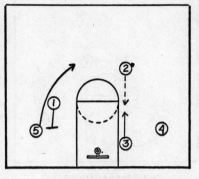

**DIAGRAM 10-11**

Another example would be if (4) is a great jump shooter. Point out to guards (1) and (2) that they should run Flex Pattern #2 quite often. See Diagram 10-12.

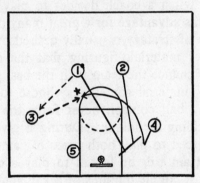

**DIAGRAM 10-12**

You can also add simple variations to utilize individual strengths. In Diagrams 10-13 and 10-14, (1) is a strong leaper. When running Flex Pattern #1 and the first cut is made, a slight adjustment is possible. Instead of (1) coming down to screen for (5), he hesitates. Then (5) comes up and blindscreens for (1), to cut to the basket for a lob pass from (2).

I believe that the numerous methods of utilizing the Flex pattern in this book will furnish many coaches with pertinent ideas for their teams.

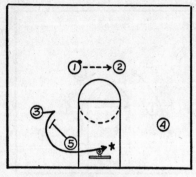

DIAGRAM 10-13

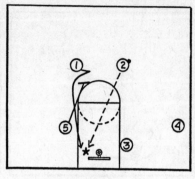

DIAGRAM 10-14

## USING THE TIME FACTOR

In basketball terminology, there are "long" games and "short" games. When a coach decides to play a "long" game, he feels it is to his advantage for a great many play situations to occur. This type of strategy is usually desired by the coach with an abundance of material, figuring that the more plays that occur, the more chance the team with the best players will win. Teams that lack material sometimes choose to play a "short" game. They play ball control, never force the fast break, and even use time-killing techniques. During a given season, most teams will be forced to play both types of games. The running, quick-shooting team will be forced to play a controlled short-type game the last couple minutes of a key game against strong opposition. The control team may fall behind to a degree, which will force them to take quick shots and do everything to increase the number of play situations. Because of these situations, any well-prepared team must have both types of offensive plays in their repertoire. A team offensive plan must be adaptable to the time factor.

To meet this requirement, this book features methods of combining the Flex pattern (a "short" game technique) with offenses that are of the "long" game nature. Examples of this are: Chapter 3, *The Flex Plus the Double Stack;* Chapter 4, *The*

*Flex Plus Set Plays;* and Chapter 6, *Auxiliary Plays,* which includes plays that offer a quick shot.

## PROVIDING FOR INDIVIDUAL INITIATIVE

The Flex is not the best offense for one-on-one players who need three or four dribbles to get into scoring position. However, the fact that the defenders must move constantly and fight through screens will allow a smart offensive player to do such things as beat his man by faking a shot and then going to the basket or pulling up for a short jump shot, or backdoor an overplaying defender. The Flex pattern converts a pressure-help type man-to-man defense into a straight man-to-man. The players should be told to stay in the pattern and look for the scoring options, but if the defense gets out of position, to react and make the appropriate basketball play. We call this disciplined flexibility.

## HAVING EASILY READ PLAY KEYS

Most offenses have four or more plays. The basic Flex offense has only two. A guard-to-guard pass keys Flex Pattern #1 and a guard-to-forward pass keys Flex Pattern #2. An apparent dilemma is that during the continuity, each subsequent sequence is called by a different player. This may involve the center or a forward starting a new play from the guard position. This situation is not as difficult as it seems at first. The constant repetition of the two basic plays is a functional teaching tool. If you are patient and a good teacher in practice, the two plays may be run interchangeably with few problems.

The first few weeks of practice should include offensive shadow drills. Five lines are used with one at each of the Flex positions. See Diagram 10-15.

The first player in each line steps out and the ball is given to a player in a guard position. You then call out, "Pattern #1, three times around." Flex Pattern #1 is then run three times around and a shot is taken. Those players then change lanes

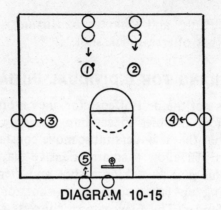

DIAGRAM 10-15

and the next five players step out. You call out, "Flex Pattern #2, three times around." This is repeated enough times so each player has an opportunity to run both of the plays from all positions.

The second step is to run the two patterns interchangeably with the man in the guard position keying either play. Explain the drill and then have your players run it three times around before taking a shot.

Third, a passive defense is used with instructions not to intercept. Three plays are run before a shot is taken.

The fourth step is to put a live defense in, but to instruct the offense to run the two plays as a stall. At this time, a half-court game is played. Team A has the ball and receives 1 point for each pass made within the context of the pattern. If a shot is taken and made, it counts 5 points. If a shot is missed, it is minus 5 points. Team A keeps the ball until Team B takes it away. Team B then plays offense. The first team to score 21 points wins the game. The losers run the bleachers five times.

The next half-court drill is to use a live defense and play games of seven. A basket counts 1 point and the scoring team gets the ball back. You call the fouls and only one free throw per foul is taken. The losers run the bleachers five times.

The next drill is a full-court controlled scrimmage and the same rules as in the previous drill are used. The teams are allowed to fast break, but after each score, the ball is given back to the scoring team.

Finally, the offense is run in a full-court scrimmage situation.

## USING BASIC PLAYS

The key basic play used in the execution of the Flex is the screen away from the ball. This is one of the hardest plays for any defense to handle. In Flex Pattern #1, the first option is post man (5)'s screen away for the offside forward (3), following a pass from the strongside guard (1) to the weakside guard (2). Most defenses expect (5)'s defender (X5) to step out (hedge) on (3)'s cut in order to give (X3) time and room to go over the top and best (3) to the onside post area. See Diagram 10-16.

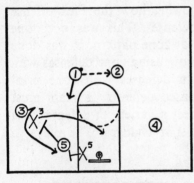

DIAGRAM 10-16

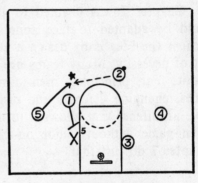

DIAGRAM 10-17

The Flex pattern takes advantage of (X5)'s hedge by having (1) come down and screen for (5)'s cut out front. See Diagram 10-17.

Pattern #2 is a double screen away by both guards (1) and (2) for the offside forward (4). There is a good chance (4) will get the jump shot. Also, this is an excellent opportunity for (3) to feed (5) in the post area since the double screen takes away the offside help. See Diagram 10-18.

The constant repetition of offside screens is very much like the passing game and is very hard to defense.

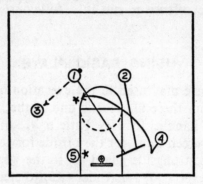

DIAGRAM 10-18

## ADAPTING TO ZONE DEFENSES

Chapter 7 was devoted to showing how the Flex offense could be adapted to face zone defenses. This was not done because the Flex is by design a great zone pattern. It was done out of necessity. Many teams are now using zone defenses with man-to-man principles, man-to-man defenses with zone principles, changing defenses and disguised defenses. A team must have an offense that allows it to meet a variety of defenses in a given game without major on-the-spot changes. The plays in Chapter 7 do just that.

## PROVIDING METHODS TO MEET PRESSURE

The Flex is a movement-oriented offense, which provides a basic pressure-relieving mechanism. The constant screening on the weak side takes away the help and makes ballside pressure very difficult. The basic problem is usually making the initial pass. If this causes too many problems, the pressure-relieving mechanisms in Chapter 6 may be used. The following pressure "killer" also works very well. Stack the onside forward ( (3) in Diagram 10-19) under post man (5) and have him utilize a downscreen to get open. At the same time, (2) screens down to allow (4) to cut to the front.

If (1) cannot make the pass to (3) or (4), he dribbles at (4). This tells (4) to make a diagonal cut. See Diagram 10-20.

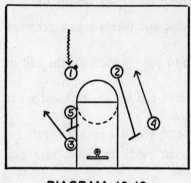

**DIAGRAM 10-19**

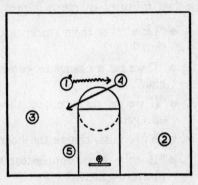

**DIAGRAM 10-20**

Player (5) steps out and (3) cuts off him. See Diagram 10-21.

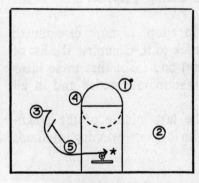

**DIAGRAM 10-21**

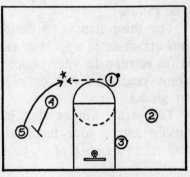

**DIAGRAM 10-22**

Then (4) screens down for (5) who cuts to the front. See Diagram 10-22.

At this point, Flex Pattern #1 is in full swing.

## CREATING TEAM EFFORT

If, by now, you are sold on the Flex and want to adopt a more disciplined attack, here is an approach to use. First, try to remember some of the instructions you have given your team in the last minutes of close games. Some examples would be:

- "Let's make them work on defense and take a high percentage shot."
- "If we get a chance to go inside to our big man, get the ball to him."
- "If we get disorganized, the guards call for the ball and set it up again."
- "If we miss, charge the boards and get us a second shot."
- "If they start double-teaming, be ready to move into our pressure offense."
- "Don't forget who is back on defense, and the rest of you hustle back if they get the rebound."
- "If we get a fast break, take it but don't force it."

The second step is to ask yourself why you did not stress these team offensive components during practice and in the easier games.

The third step is to decide to adopt a more disciplined, teamwork-oriented approach and stick to it. Complete the list of tips (in relation to your philosophy) and insist that these ideas become your team's mode of operation in practice and in all your games.

The result will be that in the last minute of the championship game, your team will have your winning methods ingrained in its style of play.

# Index